Getting Jobs in Music

CASSELL JOB GUIDES

Getting Jobs in Advertising
BY JENNY TIMBER

Getting Jobs in Beauty
BY LESLEY MOORE

Getting Jobs in Fashion Design
BY ASTRID A. KATCHARYAN

Getting Jobs in Graphic Design
BY TERRY JONES

Getting Jobs in Music
BY TONY ATTWOOD

Getting Jobs in Photography
BY KIM HOWARD

Getting Jobs in Broadcasting
BY FIONA RUSSELL

Getting Jobs Outdoors
BY MURRAY MARSHALL

Getting Jobs in Music

Tony Attwood

CASSELL

Cassell Publishers Ltd
Artillery House, Artillery Row
London SW1P 1RT

Copyright © Tony Attwood 1989

First published 1989

British Library Cataloguing in Publication Data

Attwood, Tony
  Getting jobs in music. – (Cassell job guides)
  1. Great Britain. Music – Career guides
  I. Title
  780'.23'41

ISBN 0-304-31669-5

Some occupations, titles, phrases or individual words in this publication
may refer to a worker or workers of a particular sex, but they should not be
taken to imply that the occupation or career is restricted to one sex, unless
the occupation is excluded from the general provisions of the Sex
Discrimination Act

Typeset by Scribe Design, Gillingham, Kent
Printed and bound in Great Britain by
Biddles Ltd, Guildford and King's Lynn

Contents

Contents

Who this book is for

Question: Why are you reading this book?
Answer: Because I want a job in the world of music.
Question: Yes, but what exactly do you want to do?

There are, of course, a million possible answers to that question. Here are a few to be going on with:

'I want to be...

- a composer.
- a disc jockey.
- a roadie for a rock group.
- first violin with a leading orchestra.
- one of the top superstars of the age...'

Of course no book, no individual guide, no training course, no set of mental attitudes can guarantee to give you exactly what you are after in an area of work as complex and varied as music. For a start, there are only a limited number of jobs going. Therefore there are only a small number of people who make it to the very top. So if your *only* interest in life is to be a mega-star, filling Wembley Stadium twice a year while being on good terms with Bruce Springsteen, Paul McCartney and the Princess of Wales, then don't bother with this book. If you have got what it takes, you will do it without my words of wisdom. If you haven't got that certain something possessed by the few but desired by millions, nothing I can say will ensure that you reach such dizzy heights.

If you have lesser (and more realistic) ambitions, such as playing the concert circuit, maybe even having a few hits, making acoustic guitars, working in a record company, being an ensemble player in the world of classical music, then there will be a word or two here that can help. What is more, if you know you want to be in music but you're not quite sure where your talent lies, or what your particular area of interest is, again this book can help.

You may ask, quite reasonably, can one book really deal with all aspects of music? Isn't the work of a musician in a classical orchestra so different from that of a writer of pop songs or the manager of a rock group, that there ought to be a different book for each subject? Is there really any connection between working as an arts administrator and being an orchestral composer?

Surprisingly, in one very real respect the answer is yes, there is a connection, for there is one factor that links together virtually all aspects of getting employment in the world of music. It is a factor that makes *you* different from everyone who doesn't want to be in the world of music. Here's how:

Imagine you want to be a history teacher in a school. From the moment you decide that that is the type of work you want, your path is clear. You have to get a degree and then undergo a year's training as a teacher. As that year comes to an end you will start looking around for work. This can be obtained in two ways – either you can write to the various Local Education Authorities to ask to be put on their lists of recently qualified teachers, or you can answer one of the advertisements that appear each week in *Teachers' Weekly*, the *Guardian*, or the *Times Educational Supplement*.

You will be interviewed, and in due course will get a job at a salary agreed nationally. You will not have employment guaranteed for life, but unless you do anything exceptionally stupid you can be fairly sure that your money will come rolling in for the next 40 years. What is more the structure will always be there to allow you to move jobs, get promotion (at agreed rates), take holidays (at agreed times), take paid sick leave, go on refresher courses and (if you so wish) eventually move out of the classroom into management as an adviser or head teacher.

With music everything is different

In the field of music you don't see many jobs advertised (there are a few, but not many) and certainly no one advertises for a pop songwriter or a rock group to go on tour.

There is also precious little by way of industry structure – some salaries are negotiated by unions but not many. Furthermore, there is no agreed way of getting promotion, of taking holidays, of solving problems within a job. Virtually everything is done on a person-by-person and job-by-job basis.

Many jobs in the world of music involve being self-employed. In such cases there is no sick leave, no continuing income when you need maternity leave, no income if you are a recording artist and your records suddenly flop, or if you work for a record company and they go into liquidation after having put out a string of records that no one wanted to buy.

In short, for most of the time getting into music involves being on your own in a strange land without a map.

This is a book: think of it as a map

You are after what amounts to buried treasure – a job in the world of music. Of course, you might just stumble on it, just as the treasure hunter might be walking along a beach and fall into the pit in which the gold is buried. But it is possible to increase your chances of getting the job you want by working solidly at the problem and using your map to make sense of your surroundings.

To begin with, I am not going to assume that you will know exactly what you want. So the first question you need to ask in considering your career map is:

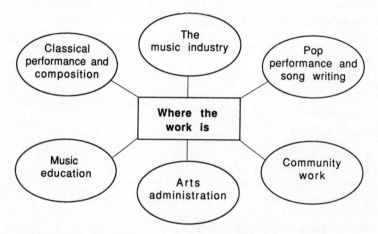

Any map that I provide can be accused of being simplistic and full of omissions. Bearing that in mind, you should consider what follows as a representation of the major areas of musical work.

Let us look in a little more detail at what each area of work offers.

Classical performance and composition

- performing in groups.
- accompanying soloists.
- performance in church.
- performing as a soloist.
- composing for specific groups, events or performances.
- playing in theatres, summer shows, etc.
- performance as a singer in shows, opera, musicals, for advertising jingles, etc.

Arts administration

- working in an established arts centre or local authority, arranging concerts, etc.

- arranging tours for artists, working as an agent (often considered part of the music industry).
- working for a record company on a classical or early music label (again strictly part of the music industry, but closely related to other arts administration).
- working for an orchestra or opera company.
- work in the sponsorship division of a large organization.

Pop performance and songwriting

- working in a pop group.
- songwriting.
- playing music for stage shows that require pop-style accompaniments to the action.

Music industry

- managing a pop group.
- promoting concerts and artists.
- arranging concert tours.
- working for a record company (this, again, can relate both to pop and classical music).
- working in a recording studio.
- selling records, musical instruments and music.
- manufacturing musical instruments.
- working in broadcasting.
- writing about music (not exactly part of the industry, although music journalists are considered to be so by many pop musicians).
- piano-tuning.
- work with firms developing acoustic equipment, loudspeakers, etc.

Music education

- working full time in a school or college.
- teaching individuals to play a particular instrument either privately or in schools, colleges, universities, etc.
- music therapy.

Community work

- work in youth centres.
- work in housing estates.
- music workshops.
- tuition outside the formal education framework.

It is already starting to look like an interesting list and yet we haven't found a place for the work of music editors, researchers, orchestral managers, copyists, librarians, radio and television producers, festival administrators, British Council staff and many, many more.

In many of the areas mentioned there are far too many people chasing too few jobs; only the determined will ever succeed. In some areas, however, the situation is reversed, for there are too few music teachers – especially at the level of individual tuition on specific instruments – and too many pupils. In piano-tuning the same applies – too few tuners and too many pianos to be tuned.

This book can help you on your way to a successful career. What *you* must provide is the guts, determination, drive and desire to succeed. (And, by the way, a little spot of talent would not go amiss as well.)

You must remember that the jobs and opportunities mentioned here are but one fraction of what people can do in music. There are thousands of people who are happily earning a living from music, having developed their own unique approach. Such people may have realized that being supertalented at school or college may not be enough to enter an orchestra. A few may move into the armed forces (the Army, Navy and Air Force all have their own music schools). The Metropolitan Police likewise have a band. Pianists are in demand everywhere, from keep fit classes to up-market restaurants.

A good colleague of mine – David Simon – added to his income by playing piano at medieval banquets held in London for American and Japanese tourists with pots of money and no knowledge of history. A Henry VIII lookalike character ran the show, and would, from time to time, break into song in any key that took his fancy. David's job was to follow him on the piano. The fact that the pianoforte was not an instrument of the period didn't seem to worry anyone. The microphone wasn't authentic Tudor either.

Other people work part time outside music as well as taking any musical work they can get. Computer programmers, accountants and secretaries all manage to combine musical and non-musical jobs without problems. But for many, where finances dictate that there must be a combination of jobs, there is a strong feeling that all the work should ideally bear some relationship to music.

1
What work is there?

I can find no better way to illustrate that musicians need actively to create opportunities than through the case of Lawrence Perkins who has combined his work as a professional musician with that of running his own business as a sound engineer. What follows is Lawrence's own story in his own words.

'I started playing the bassoon at the age of fourteen. Two years later I was accepted into the Northern School of Music, which became the Royal Northern College while I was there. The new college was quick to appoint a recording engineer – so quick in fact that John Bower took the post with virtually no recording equipment to work with. He had his own reel-to-reel machine and I had some reasonable quality microphones, and between us we made the first recording of a college orchestral concert.

Since college days I have maintained a busy schedule of solo and orchestral playing. I have been principal bassoonist in the Manchester Camerata since 1984. As a soloist I have given many concerts with my regular recital partner, pianist Michael Hancock. Together we have performed at the Wigmore Hall and Purcell Room, have made numerous broadcasts for Radio 3 and made a record for the Hyperion label (*'L'apres-midi d'un dinosaur'*) which won widespread critical acclaim and a three-star rating in the *Penguin Stereo Record Guide*.

'In 1982 I started to produce a series of special cassettes for use in conjunction with Associated Board examination studies. Tapes of this kind were controversial at the time; some teachers worried that they might be used as a 'teach yourself' cassette or that students might simply copy a recorded performance, although the literature with the tapes clearly states that this should not happen.

'In 1982, my wife, Susan Scott (also a bassoonist), and I created Sonorama, a specialist sound recording service for schools, choirs, amateur societies or any groups wishing to make a record or cassette. Applying nearly a decade of experience as a professional musician, and with a wide range of recording activities, I felt I could contribute greatly in musical production and in classical recording technique. As a 'dry' studio is both unpleasant and unsatisfactory for a choir or a string quartet to perform in, I chose to do all recordings on location, working in live acoustics.'

Anyone reading Lawrence's account of his work is bound to feel that here is someone who has devised an interesting variety of activities based around his musical abilities and interests. But just how has he managed to move from being a student to being involved in so many diverse projects?

In fact, Lawrence's first booking – a short broadcast by the local BBC radio station – was arranged for him by his college. Subsequent work as a performer came through his own efforts – Lawrence has never used a London agent. As he now admits, he started by publishing a very basic leaflet, which brought in a few bookings, and has since gone on to improve this basic piece of advertising material dramatically.

In 1978 he went further in promoting himself by making his own record and selling it through specialist shops. Although only 1,000 copies were sold, the operation did have the benefit of helping to attract Hyperion and landing that contract. As so often happens in these situations, the label manager at Hyperion said, 'Have you made any other records?' and of course Lawrence was able to say yes.

The work on the examination pieces showed just as much initiative on Lawrence's part, for he sought out the Associated Board exam syllabuses, gained copyright clearance from the various copyright owners, and then made the recordings, the tapes of which were sold through various music shops. More recently, distribution of these tapes has been taken over by a national company.

Thus, in each case we can see musical ability combined with enterprise and drive. Nothing fell into Lawrence's lap – his success comes entirely from hard work and a willingness to try out new ideas. If that all seems too much like hard work and risk, then stop reading now. The music business is not for you.

But what if, with the best will in the world, you are not fantastically talented as a musician? Do not despair – all firms need staff of one type or another: radio stations need record librarians, record companies need secretaries, rock groups need drivers, opera houses need box office personnel, the Performing Right Society needs people to look up copyright ownership, and so on. Other jobs require other forms of talent; witness the instrument builder, the music therapist, the piano tuner, etc.

No job will guarantee you promotion to higher things within the company concerned, and stories stating, 'I joined as a tea boy, never knowing that twenty years later I would be principal cello', probably owe more to Hollywood than reality. But if you are keen on music, if you are pushy, but willing to take on menial work to begin with, then an appointment within a music-related company can be a starting place. You will see how the music world works and make a few contacts.

Why are contacts important?

Many organizations within the world of music are very small – music publishers, for example, can consist of a principal, a secretary/telephonist and a couple of juniors. When a junior leaves, the principal (usually known as the managing director or senior partner) has the task of replacing 25 per cent of the work force. In making an appointment he knows that should he appoint the wrong individual, the company can grind to a halt through one person's incompetence or lack of effort. So if the principal spots a likely employee doing a menial job, and if he feels this employee is going to be reliable and competent, he will offer that person the job, being fairly sure of a greater chance of success than if he simply advertises and takes someone on interview alone.

The rule is simple: *get yourself known* by whatever means you can and *use every contact* you can find to improve your position, but do it always with a degree of discretion. There is no point in annoying potential employers by pushing too hard.

Lawrence Perkins recording a school choir.

2
Have you got the right temperament?

If there is a single message from the first chapter of this book it is this: *no job in music is ever going to fall into your lap.*

Put another way, before you start work either as a musician or within the music industry, you are going to have to work at getting the job. Quite simply, this means selling yourself. If you prefer to hide your light under a bushel then the world of music is not for you. You *must* believe you can do the job you have chosen better than anyone else. And you have to be prepared to make that opinion widely known.

But how do you know if you really do have the right sort of personality to make the grade? You may be able to psyche yourself up once or twice in order to get through the interview for the job you are after, but can you keep up the hype day after day, week after week? The personality quiz which follows should not be taken too seriously, although the issues raised should provide pointers to just how well suited you are to work in the music business. The quiz applies to all aspects of the music world except music education, which, as we have already mentioned, is different.

For each question answer either 'yes'; 'no'; 'sometimes yes and sometimes no' or 'don't know'.

1. If someone criticizes your work, does it make you feel that you are not that good at your work after all, and should possibly consider giving up the idea of working in music?

2. Do you get irritated if you have to work irregular hours and sometimes miss out on your sleep, take meals on the move, eat whatever is available rather than your favourite food and suffer from other disruptions of a settled way of life?

3. Do you feel that one of your main reasons for wanting to work in music is that you will meet a lot of famous people?

4. Do you find you can always express yourself clearly and make people understand what you are talking about?

5. Do you find it easy to relax with people you have only just met?

6. Do you think that music is the most important thing in the world?

7. Are you married or do you have a regular boyfriend or girlfriend? (Answer 'sometimes yes, sometimes no', if you don't have a regular boy- or girlfriend now, but have had in the past.)

8. Do you honestly feel you could live in less attractive surroundings in order to save money so that you can do what you really want to do?

9. Do you feel that it is important to have a really steady job with a reasonable income in order to insure against a rainy day?

10. If you are in a crowd and there is something interesting happening, do you push through to the front to make sure you get in on the act, whatever it is?

Now mark your answers from the chart below. ('Don't know' answers count the same as 'sometimes yes, sometimes no'.)

	Yes	No	Sometimes yes, sometimes no
1.	0	3	1
2.	0	3	1
3.	0	3	1
4.	3	0	1
5.	3	0	1
6.	3	0	1
7.	0	3	1
8.	3	0	1
9.	0	3	1
10.	3	0	1

The possible scores range from 0 to 30. The higher the score the more likely you are to succeed in the world of music.

Now check your score in more detail:

Score 0-10 The last thing in the world you should do is get into music. You enjoy security and home life far too much – choose a job that gives you just that. Stop reading this book now, it will only upset you.

Score 11-20 Working in the music industry might just work out for you, but you must be careful to select employment which won't lead to personal criticism, and find something with a certain amount of security. Working for a small non-pressured organization, perhaps writing sleeve notes on recordings of Balinese music issued with a

GETTING JOBS IN MUSIC

view to breaking down cultural barriers, could be viable. You might also consider work involving making traditional instruments, or perhaps piano-tuning, both low-pressure areas.

Of course you could be one of those people who succeed in the world of music despite their personality simply because you have such an enormous talent. Yet even people such as these tend to change as they continue to work in music, developing the harder outer layer which is necessary to cope with the vagaries of the industry that now surrounds music. Do you really want to change your personality, just for music?

Score 21-25 Take care – your mark looks high, and you could probably get a job in the world of music if you are determined enough. But how much you would enjoy it is another matter. Some people grow into jobs, but not everyone. Be prepared for further shocks to the system – getting the job is only half the battle.

Score 26 plus OK – you can make it, but wouldn't you prefer something a little safer, like snake charming or lion taming?

Why should success in music be so strongly related to having a particular personality? The answer is simple. For every person with a job in music there are hundreds – perhaps thousands – who have at one time or another aspired to such a job. The competition to get into music is very high indeed and naturally that breeds a certain toughness.

This is no bad thing, since the world of music is itself one of the most competitive and cut-throat areas of employment that there is, rivalled only by other communications industries such as film, advertising and television. In fact, what most people forget is that if they do succeed in getting into music, they will find themselves operating in ways quite different from those prevalent in virtually any other job it is possible to imagine.

A world unto itself

Working in music involves being in a world in which you are liable to be judged by how good you are *today*. Your success yesterday is neither a redeeming feature for those employing you, nor for yourself (if you take any pride in your achievements). Since there are hundreds of people willing to take on your job, you and they are involved in a fierce battle for survival, whether you like it or not.

In the world of music there is little formality. Everyone calls everyone else by his or her first name, but don't be misled – they will also be calling for your blood the moment something goes wrong. Most people in the business live on adrenalin, nobody gets a second chance, and, apart from a small number of star performers, producers and managers, everyone is instantly replaceable. The stars can make the odd mistake, but only the odd one. Eventually they, too, become replaceable and are faced with a dismal future known only by the tag, 'Didn't you use to be...'.

Can I really survive in such a cut-throat environment?

One way to find out is to cast yourself in certain hypothetical situations, such as:

1. You have played in a couple of concerts with a famous performer. Your part was very, very small, and you know very well that the star wouldn't know you from Adam – you were just another one of hundreds of people whom he plays alongside. Now you are up for a job. Would you let it be known that you played with the star, conveniently forgetting to point out how small your part was?

2. You have been working in a small provincial office which arranged tours of second- and third-rate acts around northern England. Your job as an office junior involved putting away files that had been left out, making the coffee, stuffing envelopes. In talking to a possible employer who is offering a job in London, would you spell out the boring truth, or state that you were in tour management with an up-and-coming out-of-town company?

3. The orchestra you played with as a student was once involved in making a TV show for a commercial station in Scotland. In fact, the orchestra was on screen for no more than fifteen seconds, and your face could just be made out for two of those seconds as a camera panned across. Would you include in your promotional literature a note which stated that you appeared on Scottish TV in 1989, with no reference to the size of your contribution?

These examples show the opportunity that all music people have of developing the truth – not exactly lying but deliberately seeking to give an enlarged impression of what one did. I am neither proposing that you *must* do such a thing in order to get a job in music, nor suggesting that everyone else does it. Rather, I am suggesting that some other people, who are seeking the same positions as you, will be using this sort of approach, although it is extraordinary how many of these exaggerations get found out. (It is a very small profession.) You may decide to fight fair, but you have to recognize that not everyone you are up against will be operating by the same rules.

In short, if you are resilient, pushy, able to communicate freely with people you don't know, persistent, hard working, reliable and totally committed to getting a job in music, you will probably get on. If, however, you despair after sending off five letters without getting a single reply, or take it personally when you 'phone to enquire about job possibilities and are told not to waste the company's time, then the world of music is probably not for you.

3
Working as a musician

Pop and the classics

In essence the difference between a pop musician and a classical performer is as much one of education as it is of musical preference. The overwhelming majority of people who work as classical musicians have been trained at university or music college. There they work closely with their tutors and their fellows, they play in college concerts, and begin to get to know people in the outside world who can help with their desire to become professionals. Small ensembles may get themselves together to play locally; particularly talented performers may catch the attention of London agents; some players may gain work as deputies in a nearby orchestra.

Once more we are in the world of 'who you know' – the contacts and experience gained as a student are put to good use by the successful musician. In those formative days at college there will always be one or two members of staff on hand to help by providing further information if the need arises. From then on contacts breed contracts; the grapevine does its job.

By contrast, in the world of pop the average performer is either self-taught or informally taught by friends, brothers, sisters and the like. As soon as guitarists can play three chords they form themselves into groups and start practising in bedrooms, garages and church halls. After a while they begin to pick up bookings at local dances. If they are any good the bookings multiply and the venues get larger until another local enthusiast offers to become their manager, taking the group further into the world of live music. Greater success can come if the manager is able to bring the group to the attention of a record company representative, or gain exposure through a competition or local broadcast of a festival or similar event.

Yet, despite the obvious differences between pop and the classics, all performers face the same problems of selling themselves and their art, and for this reason you should avoid the temptation to skip parts of this book that don't appear to relate to your type of music.

Neither the classical nor the pop performer operates in isolation. The classical student starts to pick up occasional paid performances while still at college. If he gets just one booking in a month it matters not, as he is on a grant and still studying. The pop or rock musician, on the other hand, may get his first semi-professional booking while still at school. If he goes to college he will continue to play there, and, as with the classical student at college, if he gets only the occasional bookings that will not matter too much, for there is a grant to pay for living expenses, plus studying to be done.

The major problem for musicians is the cost of equipment, and for many that means getting into debt. But all musicians should remember that there is a flourishing market in second-hand instruments and amplification equipment. You don't need the best until you are getting close to being the best! Far too many young musicians in the pop field spend far too much time worrying about the technology rather than the music. True, a mastery of the technology, combined with access to the most recent generation of sophisticated electronics, will make you sound better, but if the musical ability is not there to begin with, it will all be a waste of time.

After college

Upon leaving full-time study many would-be musicians face the same problem – a lack of funds as the grant comes to an end, and a lack of work as one tries to break into the professional circuit.

The inevitable solution is to become a semi-professional performer – one takes on whatever jobs one can get while spending all one's spare time working as a musician. Undoubtedly, such an existence leads to tensions, most particularly when the band or orchestra is set to play at the other end of the country and musicians are forced to take off half a day here and a day there in order to fulfil commitments to the band.

On the other hand, it is not all gloom and doom. The musician does not suffer as badly as the actor, who knows that any booking will almost certainly imply a full-time commitment even if it is just for a few days, hence destroying any chance of even a part-time job. If the musician takes on a job that he likes, then the job is an insurance against the music not working out. What is more, he ought to be getting money for the gigs, as well as for the job. The music should at least pay for itself (which is probably more fulfilling and certainly cheaper than spending a lot of time down at the local).

But in return for earning the money and doing what he or she likes, the musician becomes committed to a new type of discipline – a discipline which allows for no excuses. Turn up late for the office or factory and you can use explanations of the car not starting, traffic jams on the ring road or (as some students used to say when I lectured music undergraduates in Devon) 'They were moving a herd of cows across the B3482'.

Turn up late for a recording session and you have just cost somebody several thousands of pounds. In such circumstances the excuses relating to the deployment of local cattle are not normally well received.

Learning to play

Learning to play a musical instrument is an area surrounded by mythology. Here are some favourite theories – and some answers to them:

● It's impossible to learn a musical instrument unless you learn young.

Wrong – It is quite possible to learn a musical instrument at any age. There are, however, advantages in learning young:

1. As a child you are continually learning; it is a major part of life. Teachers tell you what to do in maths, English, chemistry and a dozen other subjects, and learning an instrument becomes an extension of that daily round of instruction. Adults are often out of touch with learning, and find it hard to adjust to a situation in which an outsider tells them what to do. They also find it hard to accept failure, which is a problem as failure is a part of practising. No one can play everything perfectly, instantly.

2. To learn to play a musical instrument you need to practise every day. Since students do not have to worry too much about looking after a family, earning money and the like, they have time to practise. They are often told when to practise by adults. Adults, however, find that they don't have time to practise, either because their day is already full of creative activities, or because (and this is more likely) they are used to putting their feet up and doing nothing for a fair amount of time each day. Their day is full and something must be dropped in order to make time for practising. I am certain that any adult willing to be shown, willing to practise seriously every day, and willing to learn from mistakes, can learn just as fast as a child.

● Many people are simply too unmusical to learn to play an instrument.

Wrong – Very few people are tone-deaf. In our society we have a few brilliant musicians and a few people who really can't grasp the concepts of music at all. The rest of us have the ability, if we wish, to develop and use our musical ability.

● Pop music is so facile and simple that anyone could learn to write it within a matter of hours.

Wrong – Bad pop music is facile, simple and just plain silly. But there is not much point in learning to play it anyway, since there is no money or pleasure to be had out of it. Good pop is often highly complex, or deceptively simple, and requires hours of dedication to be able to perform it well. Likewise, successful composers of pop are immersed in their music and may write thousands of songs which they reject before hitting on the odd one that becomes a winner.

● You need a really good teacher in order to learn properly.

Wrong – Good teachers are always a help, but many brilliant pop musicians and even a few classical musicians have been self-taught. There is nothing wrong in that; for many musicians recordings of the greats and help from willing friends are all the tuition needed. (On the other hand a modest performer teaching a youngster of modest talent may well result in many of the basics never being mastered at all.)

Learning to play music well enough for others to want to listen to you is not easy. If it were, we would all be able to do it, and none of us would bother to listen to any other musicians – we'd all be too busy playing to ourselves. But most reasons for not playing a musical instrument (for example, 'I wish someone had made me learn when I was young') are just excuses.

If you can play, at some stage you will have to decide just how good you are. I really do believe that we all have the ability to be excellent musicians, but we don't achieve our potential because of the intrusion of negative circumstances. These circumstances can include:

● rebelling against what parents want.
● lack of a good instrument to practise on.
● a personality clash with a teacher.
● other interests getting in the way.

Circumstances tend to dictate just how good you will be, and there is no doubt that at some stage many would-be musicians have to reconcile themselves to the fact that they are simply not going to get as far in the music business as they would like.

Of course musical failure is often dressed up as something other than a shortage of talent – a lack of 'a break', a failure to get the right agent, and a change in public taste just at the wrong moment can all be held responsible. Sometimes something more sinister is found, such as a deliberate manipulation of the music industry by powerful interests to keep new talent out and ensure total control of everything that is released on record.

It doesn't matter if people use these excuses as long as they do not remain bitter about their failure for years to come. But remember, anyone who needs to use an excuse to explain away defeat in the world of music probably did not have the right personality in the first place. You need to believe in your ability to win through – and if you suffer setbacks at any time then you have to get straight up and fight on.

Let me give you a real example. David Roundell worked semi-professionally as a rock singer. He built small groups round himself, the groups performing songs which he wrote to suit his own voice. David was known for putting together excellent bands, and for always getting good gigs. People would often say to him how lucky he was to get all the breaks that he did, and he took such jibes with a typical smile. But privately he would complain about such comments, since he felt that he got the jobs through putting himself out in order to get work. He always made himself available, he worked hard at staying in touch with people who might require his services, and he made sure that every job he did was undertaken in a professional manner.

In effect David was pitching for jobs all the time. Even at his most successful he would not get anywhere with 80 per cent of his phone calls and letters, but the remaining 20 per cent could strike lucky. The moral is simple: there is no such thing as luck in music – only hard work. If you don't put yourself about, you will not get anywhere.

Whatever your area of interest, whether you are interested in classics or pop, if you wish to be a performing musician you must ask yourself: 'What are the criteria by which I am likely to be judged?'. Being a great violinist or rock guitarist may be a help, but is unlikely to be enough. Look at two or three musicians who are successful today and whom you admire and copy the following chart and fill it in.

MUSICIAN'S NAME ....

REASONS FOR SUCCESS:

1. Musical reasons:

2. Non-musical reasons:

The reasons you have probably given – attractive outward personality, excellent technique, massive marketing budget expended, or whatever, may all be valid, but may also, to some degree, miss the point. For example, you may not have included a way-above-average ability to sight-read (which is essential among orchestral musicians), nor an ability to sing harmonies correctly first time round, which is very, very helpful for rock musicians. But such attributes are among the many that make record companies and concert promoters willing to spend a small (or large) fortune in promoting the image of a musician. It is not just the end result that matters (although that is important) but also the way in which a musician gets to that position. For the classical musician wishing to be in an orchestra the audition is an essential part of the process of getting a job. Yet auditions can be chaos – people coming and going, timings not kept to, 'phone calls interrupting proceedings, other players trying to show off in the waiting room. Can you cope with all this, keep your head and play beautifully as if nothing were wrong? If not, then start learning how to cope now.

Note: even if you are only interested in work as a classical musician, *read on*. Much of what follows also applies to work in the classical genre.

Work as a pop musician

Pop musicians progress through a range of activities – playing gigs, making records, making videos, putting in live guest appearances on radio and TV shows, playing on other people's recording sessions, and so on. Just what is done at any particular time is related to the point of development of the musician's career, rather than any form of choice or preference. Only the superstars can choose which work they undertake.

At the very start most rock groups will take any bookings they can get: youth clubs, village halls, birthday parties, literally anything. If any one factor can be said to be a prime influence during this formative stage it will be the ability of the group to rehearse. The group going nowhere starts rehearsal sessions late, spends more time fussing over amplification and technology than music, plays whatever it feels like playing, stops regularly for 'refreshments' and has rehearsal sessions irregularly at no set venue.

The band that is making a success of itself not only avoids these pitfalls but has an agreed practice routine, with a few warm-up numbers that all the members of the band know, followed by serious work on one or two new songs, perhaps followed by a run through of the complete routine for a forthcoming booking. At the same time attention will be given to the image of the group. Some will definitely try to become showbands, others will eschew this approach, but no matter how the band looks and behaves on stage an image will develop in the mind of the public. It is always better that the image is created through planning than in a haphazard way.

After a while the successful band will start to look for specific areas of work – for example, the college and university circuit. To get onto such a circuit a good manager is needed, who will probably be in touch with a booking agent. Only then might a record company offer come along. At this stage the group will be required to make whatever records the company demands through its contract, and the band will be required to go on the road, possibly touring almost full time to promote the records and develop its name. It is at this stage that many groups are obliged to make the change from being semi-professional to full-time musicians.

Going it alone
without a manager or agent

You may choose to go it alone because you don't like middlemen, or because despite your very best endeavours you have not been able to attract a manager or agent of sufficient calibre to meet your requirements. Whatever the reason, going it alone means you need to advertise yourself.

Let us start with the obvious. If you want to sell yourself, potential buyers need to know how to contact you. As an up-and-coming young musician you might be moving around quite regularly. In such circumstances you may be worried about spending a lot of money on brochures printed with an address which itself goes out of date. Not only do you not want to send out any letters with the wrong address on them, but you should remember that although many people will (sadly) throw out your leaflet as soon as it arrives, others will carefully store it for future reference. And there is nothing worse than the idea that when they try to get in touch with you six months later, you have vanished without trace.

If you are likely to move house regularly (although staying in the same city for some time, for example as a student) then you can overcome this problem by taking out a post office box number. Quite simply, your address will then be your name, your box number and the city.

Alternatively, you can ensure that you take out redirection notices for all your post each time you move – for a small fee the Post Office will then forward your mail as required to your next address, and you will still get your communications.

Telephone numbers can be more of a problem. 'Phone numbers can be redirected or reallocated (although this is not possible on all exchanges), but if you are sharing a flat with a few others they will not want you to take the 'phone number with you when you move on, and if you are renting the landlord will probably not permit it.

Under such circumstances you can take any of the following courses of action:

1. Remember to remail everyone each time you move, pointing out your new number.

2. Put on your leaflet a second 'phone number which you know will be good for some time (parents for example, or married friends who have recently acquired a mortgage and who look like staying put for a while). Then, if someone can't reach you on the first number, they will, with luck, try the second and get your latest location that way.

If you are sharing premises with others who have no interest in your career, do remember that they may not give a particularly good impression if they answer your 'phone. Try to explain to other inhabitants of your digs how important the 'phone is to you and make sure that a pen and paper are always left by the 'phone to ensure that messages are written down as they come in.

Although it may seem an expensive luxury it will certainly be worth considering purchasing an answering machine so that calls to you do not go unanswered while you are out studying, performing or working in some non-musical job.

Selling yourself

You have a product; it has to be marketed properly.

That may sound like a set of instructions to be found in a manual from the Harvard Business School, but it applies equally to musicians who wish to be successful.

Does that disturb you? Do you feel that it somehow reduces the validity of your art to express it in the terms of the market place?

If the answer is yes, you are upset by the opening statement of this section, then you have a problem, for unless you happen to be one of the top ten musicians in the world at any one moment, you must be prepared to market yourself or else face a life which may be full of music, but which will be lacking in paid employment.

Finding work involves self-publicity, and self-publicity will only work if you adopt a clear and concise strategy from the very start. The first principle that you must learn is that you are the product and your market is a whole range of managers, agents, bookers, social secretaries and fixers who control live music in the UK.

Let us try to see how well you can cope with this aspect of the work through the following questions:

1. Do you feel unhappy about the fact that you will have to deal through a wide array of middlemen before you can get to your audience?

2. Does the thought of sending out a press release written by yourself, and describing yourself as one of the most exciting prospects of recent years, fill you with embarrassment?

3. Are you a good administrator and keeper of notes and information?

4. Would you rather be seen dead than to be heard describing music as a product?

5. Can you write a good sales letter?

6. On the 'phone do you get flustered, wishing perhaps that the 'phone did not ring so much?

7. Would you feel nervous or relaxed if suddenly asked to participate in a radio discussion programme that was going out live?

8. Irrespective of what you think of journalists, do you think you are able to work with them?

9. Are you willing to allow yourself to be described as the best performer of a particular type of music even though you know there are others better than you who, for some reason or other, are simply not getting the breaks?

10. If you saw a newspaper cutting about yourself that was highly complimentary, but totally untrue, what would you do about it?

There are no correct or incorrect answers to such questions, but you will be able to judge from what has already been said what set of attitudes is likely to give you the publicity you will need as a musician.

Having decided that you are willing to enter the market place, what should you do next? Many people try to short circuit any discussion on this point by saying 'get a manager'. This, of course, is not a real answer, because unless you are one of the very, very best musicians around at present, no manager will take you on until you have done something to prove yourself. You need to get the first few bookings on your own. Even if you have never played professionally, you have been to school and college somewhere, local societies exist near where you live now, and between them these various bodies ought to be able to give you some sort of chance. Exploit all your personal contacts, get in touch with every organization that has anything to do with your area of interest, plough through every reference book the library can offer to find more possible organizations, and then follow this research up with the production of a biography which can be used to inform the outside world just who you are.

The biography

Once you have played a few dates it is time to prepare the biography – one of the most important items in the musician's armoury.

Selling yourself or your group means communicating. What you need to reveal about yourself can be broken down into various sections: what you do, who you are, what you have done, what you look like, what other people have said about you, and so on. The divisions may not always be sharp and clear, but the general information needs to be included in the publicity you distribute in a distinct and easily read form. Subdividing your text under headings always helps.

Remember that you will often be sending out information to people who are not especially interested in you. You may catch them on a bad day, they may be busy or just plain tired. Make it easy for your reader by setting out the information clearly. If working at the simplest level of photocopied typed sheets, use double spacing and wide margins. Remember, the person reading your blurb doesn't know you and (at least to begin with) may not want to know you.

In what follows we take an imaginary rock band as the example. Although the details to be put together by an individual classical performer will be different, the nature of the information will, nevertheless, be similar. Additional sections that would be relevant only to classical musicians are listed at the end of the example.

Although the biography of the classical performer will supply the same type of information, he or she will also need to include information under:

- training
- competitions and awards
- repertoire

Note that repertoire should not be included if you are applying for work with an orchestra; the orchestra can hardly be expected to base its performances around pieces you can play!

WHAT ARE WE?

We are CIRKUS DEATH WISH, a five-piece heavy metal band plus three-girl dance group playing a combination of original songs with established heavy metal numbers. The band is available for work throughout northern England, north Wales and southern Scotland.

WHO ARE WE ?

The band and dance group met as students at Newcastle Polytechnic in 1989. All members of the troup are native to the North East.

The band consists of:

John Fellows (bass guitar/vocals)   Age 21
Robert Barton (guitar)   Age 22
Mike Feelgood (percussion)   Age 21
Dave Heap (keyboards)   Age 23
Peter Swanwick (guitar/vocals)   Age 21

The dance group consists of:
Sarah Mellows   Age 19
Susie Fitzsimmons   Age 20
Beth McKenzie   Age 20

CIRKUS Death Wish

~~WHA~~T HAVE WE DONE SO FAR?

~~CI~~RKUS DEATH WISH have performed at clubs throughout north ~~Engla~~nd and southern Scotland, including:

~~Fe~~lix Kept on Walking (Manchester)
~~Th~~e Original C (Liverpool)
~~Joh~~nny's (Newcastle)
~~Th~~e Saint (Hull)
~~Arrg~~aaah!!! (Edinburgh)

~~T~~he band has also taken part in both the fourth and fifth National Rock ~~Fes~~tivals.

~~Ra~~dio performances – we have appeared live on Radio City and Radio Tees.

~~TV~~ – The band was featured in 1988 on Tyne Tees TV programme Deadlines.

~~A~~ full list of appearances is given separately.

~~W~~HAT THEY SAID ABOUT US

'Lively to the point of being frantic, outrageous – but just the right side of ~~d~~ecency...' (Hull Echo)

'Most promising act we've seen this year.' (Manchester Evening News)

'I just hope someone books them again before their price goes up, as it ~~i~~nevitably will.' (Newcastle Chronicle)

'If they don't run out of energy first they must break nationally.' (Sounds)

'I presume the management of the Municipal Centre have now learned their lesson and will never again book such an obscene act.' (Scarborough News)

COST AND MANAGEMENT

CIRKUS DEATH WISH are available for £400.00 per evening. All enquiries to New Wave Management, 21 Park Street, Newcastle-on-Tyne. Tel: (0202) 999111

It will be noticed that our imaginary rock band used one negative as well as several positive reviews. They could get away with this because of the implications of the review. Their act is clearly lively – one reviewer commented on it as being just on the right side of good taste. In Scarborough, however, they clearly did offend at least one person – the reviewer! Yet the suggestion is that the problem arose from a different concept of decency holding sway in the critics' office of the local paper in that town, rather than problems within the act. In a humorous way the inclusion of this review says, 'The ultra-sensitive should not book us.'

Reviews of the type used here help to set the scene easily. Naturally, questions of decency do not normally affect classical musicians (nor, to be fair, do they affect the vast majority of pop musicians) but if it is possible to use a balance of positive and negative reviews, this can work well. For example, one reviewer who says, 'Contemporary music at its very best' needs to be used. But if another reviewer has also said, 'Quite what the point is of all this noise is totally beyond me', that too could be quoted as this would suggest that the problem may be with the critic rather than the musicians.

What you must seek to avoid is anything that resembles blandness. 'A promising young talent' is by and large useless. In this business you must either be brilliant or terrible (and preferably the former).

Lastly, when the text is prepared you must consider the typesetting and printing. Typesetting – the putting of your words onto the page in a format ready to be printed (known as camera-ready copy) – is often as expensive as the printing itself.

At this stage you may want to reduce costs, possibly because you are short of money, possibly because this will be your first biography and you know that in a short while there will be many details which you will need to change. There are two ways of saving money. Firstly, you can avoid typesetting by typing all the details neatly and carefully on an electric typewriter. If you do this, remember to leave a lot of space around your words (nothing puts people off more than a crowded format) and make the result look attractive. Remember, printing will merely reproduce the copy you provide – it won't make it look any better.

Secondly, use Yellow Pages and local magazines to locate an inexpensive printer. Get three or four quotes for your printing job, and note that High Street franchised printers (known as fast printers or instant printers) will often want to charge double the rate of the two-man team working out of a small factory on an industrial estate.

What you look like

In addition to all the written information presented in the biography, you should provide people interested in booking you with a couple of photographs. They need to be black and white, clear, a reasonable size (8 × 10 in (20 × 25 cm) appears to be an industry norm), professional-looking and should reflect the image you wish to present on stage. That doesn't mean they all have to be of you in action at the keyboard or whatever, although at least some of them should. If you are projecting the image of a family entertainer, then one picture taken at home, playing with the children, might mix in well with two of you on stage.

If you do go to a professional photographer, for goodness sake make sure that he or she is fully aware of the image you are looking for. Certainly, a professional is going to charge more, but the photographs will be good, are more likely to be used, and one session will give you a range of options to choose from. Remember, the pictures are not only intended to give people who are booking you a chance to see what you look like, they are also intended to be used in local newspapers and magazines, both for previews and in reviews after the event.

Make sure that you keep a stock of these promotional photos ready for anyone who wants them, and get them redone regularly – once every couple of years at least. Saying 'I've got some pictures but they're a bit dated' is just as bad as having no pictures at all!

The classics – where the work comes from

Classical musicians find their initial work in one of two ways – either as a member of an orchestra, chamber group or opera company, or as a solo performer. For some it will be possible to go straight into an orchestra or opera company from college. For every one else who doesn't manage this, the early days will be a struggle.

Some trained classical musicians have agents, but unless you have had some success already you are unlikely to find an agent who is willing to put himself or herself out for you. Indeed, even if you do get an agent you should never give up looking for work yourself – simply make sure you let your agent know what you are up to.

Would-be classical musicians will now ask two questions. Firstly, where are the opportunities? Secondly, how can the work be secured?

The first answer is that there are the **non-competitive festivals** which will be of interest to soloists and chamber musicians. The *British Music Yearbook* lists around 200 in the UK alone.

Obviously many of the festivals listed are in London, ranging from events such as the National Festival of Music for Youth to the Almeida International Festival of Contemporary Music and Perform-ance. Outside London there is also an amazing variety. The first town

listed in the *Yearbook* – Aberdeen – has four annual events: the
Aberdeen Scottish National Orchestra Summer Proms in May, the
Aberdeen Bon-Accord Festival in June, the Aberdeen International
Youth Festival in August and the Aberdeen Alternative Festival in
October. Although there are one or two notable gaps, such a diversity
of opportunity is repeated throughout much of the UK.

The variety that can be found at some of these festivals is
enormous. The Rhymney Valley Arts Festival in Mid Glamorgan, for
example, is listed only by its name and address in the *British Music
Yearbook*, and yet the festival consists of concerts, drama, opera,
lectures, art and craft exhibitions, photographic exhibitions, a young
musicians' competition and a young composers' forum.

Next there is the **education** sector. Many schools have diminutive
music departments that can't even manage to get an orchestra
together let alone arrange a concert for outside guest performers. But
there are other schools for whom music is one of the mainstays of
educational life, and these are worth contacting. Don't assume that
private schools are invariably more music-orientated than state
schools – some private schools spend so much time getting their
charges through Common Entrance, GCSE, A-level and Oxbridge
entrance exams that there is no time for what they see as the extras,
such as music. Others spend so much time on sport that, again, music
has to take a back seat.

Most public libraries contain reference books full of lists of schools
which also contain details on which subjects the schools specialize
in. The *Parents' Guide to Independent Schools*, published by SFIA
Educational Trust, is particularly helpful here, as is the *British Music
Education Yearbook*. Colleges, universities and polytechnics are also
worth contacting either through the music department, or through
the music society or students' union. And don't forget your own
college – most colleges with any sense of continuity will welcome
back old students.

Thirdly, many **music clubs and societies** flourish throughout the
UK – the *British Music Yearbook* has twelve pages of listings – and,
naturally, many are interested in booking musicians. Often these
organizations are very impoverished and are therefore forced to book
in younger musicians who are just starting out and who are (not to
put too fine a point on it) cheap.

Next we come to **local authority promoters**, who are charged with
the responsibility of running halls, theatres, etc., which are owned by
the local authority. They have a dual responsibility – bringing a wide
range of entertainment to the local populace, and making financial
ends meet. Thus, they don't have to ensure a full house for each and
every performance, but they do have to watch the budget. A list
appears in the *British Music Yearbook*.

Radio and TV are often a disappointment for young performers. Once you have started making your way in the world of music, however, it *is* worth writing to the head of music at all TV companies, to BBC national and regional radio and to the very largest commercial stations, such as Capital and Clyde, in order to try to get an audition, or be put on their lists for particular specialities that you have.

Local radio is a different affair. Local radio stations do not, by and large, arrange concerts and recitals of classical music, outside of occasional sponsored events or a couple of concerts by well-known ensembles.

However, there can be exceptions, and those exceptions can be exploited by performers writing to their own local stations. The whole point is that local stations are supposed to reflect the locality, and if you can get even a brief spot on a local arts programme it will not only help you to get known in your area, it will help you to get further bookings, for nothing impresses as much as being able to inform people that you recently had a performance broadcast on Radio XYZ.

Competitions

Whether we like it or not, for the young classical musician competitions play a major part in getting into music. This is not new – I can recall, as a twelve-year-old, attending a hall along with twenty other hopefuls, each of us playing through the same piece (now mercifully forgotten) in front of a panel of three local musical worthies. And as if that were not enough, the panel then asked four of us to play the piece all over again. For the winning three there were certificates, and for the rest a combination of resentment, humiliation, anger and determination to do better next time.

Presumably the point of this, and all the subsequent competitions for which I was entered, was that were my performances to prove to be of a high enough standard then I would continue to enter competitions in order to get better at competitions in order to enter more competitions ...

For the brilliant performer competitions can be a bonus – a way of getting noticed rapidly – for the others, it really depends once again on personality. I hated the whole process, even though I did rather well, in the early years at least. Competitions were the one thing that made me nervous on stage; I felt physically sick for at least two days beforehand (although my recovery was instantaneous after the event). But for others competitions do offer a series of targets to reach, plus a chance to gauge oneself against the opposition. The only problem is that there is no guarantee that the judges will really have any reasonable idea of what are, and what are not, good techniques and performance.

As general rules, I would offer the following to would-be competitors.

When to compete (and when not to compete)
● If you can stand it, enter a few competitions each year.
● Avoid making competitions the only musical activities you indulge in.
● Try to choose competitions run by recognized authorities and organizers.
● If you find yourself in a competition which is disorganized, or badly run, see it through but make sure you do not take part in any other events organized by the same people.
● Only enter competitions that will give you worth-while experience, even if you lose. For example, there is no point in entering a competition on a stage in a small county town in front of the local dignitaries if you are already fully experienced at playing in local authority halls.
● Ensure that the prizes are worth having. Where possible, start with events which offer a range of small prizes rather than one big prize, since that way you stand a greater chance of coming out with a profit.
● Don't enter any competitions before you are ready. Any decent competition will be back next year, or the year after. Don't rush yourself – it will do neither you nor your career any good.
● Make sure you are playing pieces that you are good at and which will impress the judges.
● Check out the judges. Do you trust them to make a reasonable decision? If not, forget it!
● Apply in good time and treble check your entry form. About 50 per cent of all entry forms either arrive late or are filled out incorrectly.

Perhaps one may finish with a brief mention of three interesting competitions which themselves may be used as benchmarks against which others may be judged.

For young pop and rock musicians there is the TSB Rock School administered by the Trotman Group of companies based in Richmond, Surrey. This competition has the advantages of being one of the few for young rock musicians, and being long-lived, which normally means that most of the problems have been ironed out!

For young classical musicians there is the Young Musician of the Year which has the overwhelming advantage of being organized by BBC TV, and thus gaining massive television coverage each year. It is interesting to note that after the winners are announced many music societies, clubs and orchestral societies write in to the BBC asking if they may engage winners from various classes. Meetings are then held with winners, their parents and teachers to help winners choose which engagements they feel would be most advantageous to their continuing development.

Finally a more recent competition, the Audi Junior Musician for players between twelve and sixteen, is an event supported by the Royal College of Music. This competition has the advantage that all participants receive a plaque, and the winners of each round, including the first, receive a prize. The outright winner appears as a soloist at a special public performance with the Royal College of Music.

Opportunities for classical singers

I can't recall ever having met a classical singer who was not aiming for the very top – a career as a soloist. While bass players in rock bands and clarinettists in orchestras often feel quite satisfied with the possibility of a long-term future in a professional rock band or orchestra, the singer typically wants the limelight. Chorus work is seen as a failure.

This is a great problem, for the amount of solo work available is tiny in the extreme – the failure rate (as measured by those singers who end up in the chorus or, worse, without a professional singing job at all) is massive.

And yet it is clear that no words of warning, either from me or anyone else, are liable to put singers off. So what should a hopeful singer do?

Firstly, take the best training on offer, and develop your voice to its maximum potential within its own style. Do not fall into the trap of believing that the best singing comes naturally. Training may not be essential in rock bands (although it can be helpful), but for the classics you cannot escape it. Remember it takes years and years for a classical voice to develop fully; some classical singers are still supplementing their income from other sources into their thirties.

Secondly, make sure you are physically fit. Remember, a violinist can still play beautifully with a sore throat, and can even cope with a bruise on the wrist, but the endless round of bugs and viruses that have become part of living in the sanitized late twentieth century will ensure time off work for all but the fittest singers.

Thirdly, consider your own personality. Such a piece of advice for a rock singer will raise a few laughs, since no one can contemplate singing rock music without having the type of personality that will be attractive to audiences. But while the 'act' is seen as part of the show by rock musicians, the classical musician may resist, preferring instead to argue that 'the music is the thing' and that the audience should not be distracted. Such thoughts may be laudable, but they will not earn you work. Our society wants extroverts as singers whether you like it or not.

Next, once you have your voice trained and your on-stage personality sharpened, be prepared to work your way around auditions. Advertisements appear continually in the music press, and your teacher should also be able to point you in the right direction. If you don't know which journals to read, go to the periodical section of your nearest major public library – some will be in stock there and the librarian will also be able to guide you towards other relevant titles.

From then on it is a case of doing as much work as possible: college concerts, operatic choruses, end-of-the-pier summer seasons, winter cruises to the Caribbean. If the offer is there, take it.

Music in church

Many religious establishments do put on concerts as well as offering regular work for organists; some also have professional choirs. They may not pay much, if anything at all, but such opportunities are worth looking into. Even if remuneration is small, such possibilities may be worth pursuing simply to increase your experience and the list of places you have played, as shown on your CV. Remember that at the start of a career all experience is worth while (and you never know who may be listening).

Setting up an ensemble

This isn't as difficult as you may at first think. You don't need anyone's permission, there are no forms to fill in; you just recruit the musicians and start to rehearse.

Yet many ensembles fail, not because of lack of bookings (although this is often a factor) but because the original creator of the ensemble has not laid down the ground rules. When joining together with friends and friends of friends, a lot may be taken on trust, and it is not until some time later that questions may be raised on issues which you have always taken as read.

It is better to agree on fundamentals before you begin, such as the type of music you will play, the division of the spoils, the payment of the cost of promoting yourselves and, most painfully of all, who takes the decision to deal with the member of the group whose work is simply not up to standard.

Finance and status

There are a few technicalities surrounding the forming of an ensemble. It is certainly best to open a bank account in the name of the ensemble, as this will make the financial status of the group easy

to understand, both from the point of view of the tax man and the ensemble members. It is also possible to form the ensemble into a charity, which will help in the gaining of grants and awards (but check first to see how much the solicitor's fees will cost).

Some people suggest setting up as a limited company, on the grounds that this will ensure that one or two individuals are not caught with large debts if the ensemble gets into financial difficulty. In my view this is an error. The tax position for limited companies is normally much harsher than for non-limited companies and certainly the preparation of the annual accounts is a much more expensive affair. What is more, when organizations do get into trouble, the main body they owe money to is normally the bank, but banks will only give overdrafts to organizations on the condition that one or more individuals guarantee the loan. Hence, if you are the guarantor you will be caught for the debts whether your ensemble is a limited company or not.

All in all, it is better to put in charge of the accounts of your ensemble someone who is at least numerate or, better still, has the ability to read and prepare a balance sheet and profit and loss account.

There is no need to register for VAT until the turnover of your ensemble goes above the basic VAT limit which, after the 1988 Budget, stood at £22,100. I stress that this is the turnover, not the profit of the ensemble – if you invoice out over £22,100 in the course of one financial year your ensemble *must* register for VAT. (But note that certain grants may not count towards this figure – your accountant or the local Customs and Excise office will give you the details.)

Below that level you can choose to register or not. Registering has the effect of increasing the amount you have to charge for a concert by the level of VAT (15 per cent in 1988). However, if the organization booking you is itself registered for VAT, it will then claim that money back, so it won't mind paying the extra 15 per cent. Only if you are regularly being booked by very small societies, with turnovers of under £22,100, will your VAT charge be a problem.

On the other hand, there are advantages for your ensemble in registering, in that if the ensemble spends any money on petrol, instrument repairs, accommodation, and the like, then the 15 per cent VAT included in the bill can be reclaimed from Customs and Excise.

Customs and Excise put out numerous booklets to help newly registered organizations, but remember one particular thing before jumping eagerly into VAT registration. Some additional book-keeping is involved, not least keeping a copy, in strict date order, of each invoice issued and each invoice received. Do you really want to do that?

Working through orchestral agents

When looking for work in orchestras, it is helpful to get in touch with orchestral fixers. By far the most appropriate course here is to scan the *British Music Yearbook* and choose the correct fixers for you.

With some smaller orchestras you are unlikely to be offered an audition – any offers you do get will be for immediate work. Bearing this in mind you should write to the fixers you have chosen, setting out clearly the following information:

- who you are and what instrument you play.
- where, when and under whom you studied.
- what prizes you have won.
- what experience you have had in other orchestras.
- any bookings you currently have.

With that information you should offer to supply a cassette and a photograph of yourself. What you should *not* include is a rambling letter, details of how well you did at maths A-level, or how you are not only a brilliant percussionist but also play the viola quite well. It will not enhance your attempt to convince a fixer of your ability, and could seriously diminish your chances.

Musicians' Union and other organizations

In some cases musicians are virtually obliged to join representative organizations – orchestral players are always in the Musicians' Union; operatic performers are normally in Equity. In other cases performers may join an organization if they wish, but the matter is entirely one for the individual to decide. Many, but not all, classical musicians are in the Incorporated Society of Musicians.

Some groups are served by several conflicting bodies; teachers, for example, may join the National Union of Teachers, the Association of Schoolmasters/Union of Women Teachers or any one of about half a dozen other unions. Some join the Musicians' Union.

Composers need to protect their copyright and for this reason they join the Performing Right Society and the Mechanical Copyright Protection Society. Instrumentalists tend to have their own societies for their own instruments – for example, the Incorporated Association of Organists, the British Flute Society and so on.

Why should anyone join any of these societies? Different societies offer different advantages ranging from various forms of insurance to discounts in various shops, from protection of earnings to ways of meeting like-minded professionals. Remember, it is always worth seeing what each society has on offer, especially since fellow members of the right society may provide exactly the contacts you need in your search for information and work as a performer.

Getting your music recorded

How to get onto record? Simply follow these rules:
● If at all possible get an agent or manager who knows the ropes and will arrange the technicalities for you.
● If you can't get a manager, work your way through a current record catalogue, noting down the recording companies issuing music of the type that you perform.
● Use *Music Week Directory* or *Kemps* to find the addresses of the record companies.
● Get a professional recording made, either using your own portable studio or in a professional recording studio.
● 'Phone the first company on your list and discover the name of the producer to whom tapes should be sent.
● Send a brief CV, with the tape, to that producer, making sure that your name and address is on the tape as well as on the letter.

There is a 99 per cent chance that this approach will fail, not because the method is wrong but because there are too many people seeking too few recording opportunities. However, all is not lost for it is quite possible for individuals to use the recordings made and have records pressed from them; details of the various organizations that undertake the manufacture of records on a small scale are given in the *Music Week Directory*. Indeed, if you have the money, or can borrow it from the bank, you will find the making and packaging of your own record is not at all difficult.

The problem lies in the selling of the resultant product. Of course, there will be many copies you will actually not want to sell, but will give away to impress others who might book you; a record with a proper sleeve and a picture of yourself on the back is an impressive achievement, even if you own the 'record company' that produced the music.

But you *will* want to sell other copies, and these can be distributed through specialist music shops, especially the ones in your own locality where you may be known, and at venues where you are playing. All you need is a colleague to set up a stall in or around the entrance foyer, with a pile of your records and a bag in which to put the money!

A middle way between a fully blown recording contract and a recording made by yourself comes with the sponsored recordings. A recording is a tangible item, and it is often easier to get a sponsor for such a project (which can, of course, bear the sponsor's name) than for the less tangible concert. More details on sponsorship will be given later.

For many rock groups the making of a record can be a major breakthrough, but for many others the hoped-for income never quite develops. There can be several reasons for this:

● The records might not take off. Far too many records are released each year – only a fraction of them become hits. Record companies are often willing to live with failure for a few records if the group is having success on the road and developing a style which might lead to success later. But this is not always so, and record contracts can be cancelled. A group that has had a contract cancelled is normally finished; there are many other performers around who will want to replace them. For the individual musicians involved this may well be a time to think again, perhaps breaking up and re-forming with different personnel, a different image, a different style ...

● The expenses may exceed the income. To tour professionally, perhaps as a warm-up act to the recognized star on a national tour, often means buying in new equipment. The record company may loan a group the money required for this, or may make an advance out of the expected income on forthcoming records. This invariably means that the group will be left with little to live on, with the national tour being undertaken in a dilapidated van (no chaffeur-driven Rolls drawing up to allow the band to push through adoring fans), with the group staying at third-rate hotels, eating fish and chips, and having no spare cash to put aside for later. Articles on the group may appear in *New Musical Express* and *Melody Maker* and the record may start to climb the charts, but none of that means that more money will be immediately available to the group – remember, it all went on the equipment.

● Members of the group may find that although they can get on together on a part-time basis, living out of each other's pockets 24 hours a day does not always make for peaceful co-existence. The strains of living close together on a record-promoting tour can be enough to lower the quality of the music being played. Eventually the group might even break up. One member might possibly be replaced without the band sinking, but if the group splits in half it can be hard going to put everything back together again. When arguments develop as to which half of the group owns the right to continue with the contract issued by the record company, you know you are in trouble.

● If the band does stay together, there will then be radio interviews, TV appearances, video work, more records, more live appearances and so on – with the schedule still dominated by the requirements of the record company and management rather than the wishes of the musicians. Only much later can the individual performers start to determine exactly which way they want their careers to go, and then only if they have the magic ingredients:

Fame and talent

You can achieve success from fame without talent. This is based on the concept of hype, that is, the building up of the image of a record or a musician through well-planned and cleverly organized publicity, but with little regard for the true artistic merit of the music. It can work for a while, although eventually you will be found out for what you are – no better or worse than everyone else. Talent without fame can be frustrating if you cannot get a foothold on the ladder of success, but for those with the energy and determination to work their way up, talent will always be recognized for what it is.

But chart success is not everything. Frank Zappa, one of the most successful and most enduring of rock musicians has maintained a career for over 25 years without one hit single in either America or Britain. Yet he was as able to fill the largest stadia in the UK during a tour in 1988 as he was in 1968. The fact is that Zappa has carved out a unique niche for himself within the musical world, and fans will travel great distances to see him. Originality on its own is not enough, but originality plus talent can once again secure a long-term future in the music world.

When you get a job

It doesn't matter if it is in the field of pop or the classics, the rules which apply are simple:

- be on time.
- don't waste anyone else's time.
- don't show off.

That all seems very simple, but when you do get work in an orchestra or as a soloist or play in a rock band, take a moment to watch some of the other performers, and count just how many *are* breaking the rules.

After the show is over make sure you:

- Talk to everyone who wants to talk to you. The time for saying you don't talk to youngsters who want to know how to become musicians may come later (although I hope it never does).
- Accept all comments in good grace. At the very least say, 'I'll bear

that in mind' and have the courtesy to recognize a good idea when you hear one.

- After each event write a letter of thanks to the organizers, expressing your desire to return when a suitable occasion arises (although there is no need to do this if you were playing with an orchestra).

Press cuttings

There are many agencies which will look out for and forward press cuttings for you. Mostly they are listed in theatrical and musical reference books and in Yellow Pages. Press cutting is an expense that you may feel you can do without in the early days, but once you have made a large number of appearances, and particularly if you are on radio or TV and making a record, you may find that you wish to have a press cutting agency look after your interests. The idea is that every time your name appears in print you will get to know about it, so the simple rule is only sign up and pay your money if:

● you think your name is likely to appear quite often.
● when you get the press notices you will do something with them.

By this I mean make quite sure that you actually need more notices for your promotional material. Ask yourself: are they going to be useful? If not you may be paying out a lot of money for pure vanity.

Sponsorship

Sponsorship looks attractive to any forlorn artist wondering how he or she is going to make it in the world of music. It is also a very difficult area to crack, for most businesses which are looking to sponsor the arts will only do so in order to:

● enhance their image by being associated with the arts in general
● be associated with quality and/or success
● ensure their name is in front of an important and discerning section of the public.

If you are unknown in the world of the arts then you are going to have difficulty in convincing a would-be sponsor that what you are doing is going to be of a high enough quality to warrant sponsorship. Turn your thoughts away from the sponsorship of you to the sponsorship of your event. For example, you may know of a small yearly festival which is willing to engage you to play, but which suffers from a disastrous lack of funding. Alternatively, there may be a tour of concerts, or perhaps a competition. These could well be things that a local firm would be willing to have its name associated with, especially if musicians of some stature are willing to put their names to the event.

Next, present your plans for sponsorship to suitable firms at least six, and preferably twelve, months ahead of the event or tour. Describe your idea and outline what the sponsor will get out of it – mentions in the programmes, association through the name of the festival being changed, local radio coverage, free tickets to events and the like. (You will never be able to guarantee local radio coverage for an event one year away, but if you can show that you have had serious discussions with the programme controller at your local station, and can give his/her name as a reference which the sponsor may follow up, then that can certainly help.)

In addition you should outline how much money you want. Never suggest you will take anything you can get, but do allow for variance – perhaps asking for £5,000 for the sole right to sponsor a tour as it is currently planned, but with the allowance that the sponsor can require additional advertising to that already planned, so long as he is willing to pay for it.

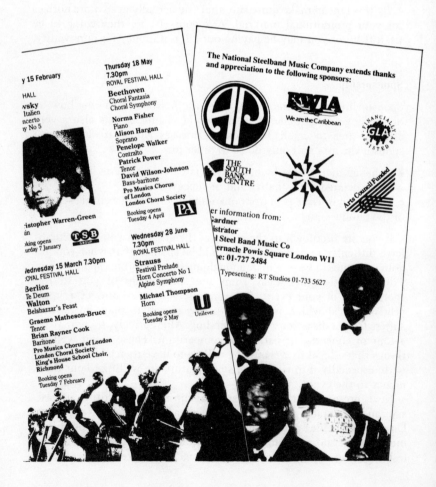

Sponsorship research

Various organizations and publications exist which can help you in your search for a sponsor. Any list which might be printed here would run the risk of being out of date by the time the book is published, therefore it is better to offer general sources from which you can obtain more information.

Firstly, the Office of Arts and Libraries, which houses the Minister for the Arts, holds information on business sponsorship schemes. Secondly, the Arts Council themselves publish a helpful guide on the subject. Thirdly, your nearest major public library will have a reference section which should contain various directories on major companies, and possibly a volume or two on sponsorship. Finally, there is the Business Sponsorship Incentive Scheme which is run by the Association for Business Sponsorship of the Arts, for the Minister. The Association can be reached at 2 Chester St, London SW1X 7BB.

Having explored the background it is worth drawing up a short list of possible sponsors. Don't pick names out of a hat, but look for links. Watch out for anniversaries of foundation, local connections, companies already involved in some sponsorship, but none that is directly competitive with what you are trying to do. Then, having made your short list and prepared a suitable brochure, telephone the company to obtain the name of the person to whom you should send your material, and also send a brief, but personal, covering letter. Do not photocopy the covering letter; you are offering something unique, not selling ice cream!

When the success stops

It may seem rather premature to talk about the end before you have even begun, but initial, or even moderately long-term success can come to an end before you would like it to. The reasons for the end of success are various – they may be physical; a broken wrist that never properly mends, damaged vocal cords, etc. They may be psychological – the strain of an endless round of concerts and recordings is enormous. They may be a reflection in changing taste – a decline in the level of bookings you get as younger talents with more energy, and wanting less money, come onto the scene. In the world of pop you may fall by the wayside as, following a string of hits, your style loses its appeal and your record company loses its interest in you.

Given that as a performer you will have been self-employed, you can expect little benefit or help from the state unless you are truly destitute. It is therefore essential that you rapidly find yourself alternative employment.

The one thing that the ex-performer has on his or her side is the range of contacts made in the music world. This can result in the offer of a job in the music industry, or a chance to move from performance into songwriting or other areas of composition. Some performers may choose to work in management, seeking out new talent, while others move away from the industry and prefer to go into private teaching. A good friend of mine moved from being something of a rock star to being the programme controller of a radio station.

Clearly all these jobs build on the experiences of the performer. When the work is no longer coming in it is easy to see one's past as a failure to scale the heights and remain at the summit, but this need not be so, for all performers build up a wealth of knowledge which can be used in subsequent work.

Think positively – in music there is no alternative!

4
Composition

If the general problem with working in the world of music is that there are far too many people who want to do it, then this applies doubly to composition. A tiny, tiny number of lucky souls manage to earn a full-time living out of composition. For the rest composition must remain a part-time (and often amateur) activity. Fortunately, composition is something that can normally be integrated into other musical work. If you are working as a soloist, a teacher, or an orchestral performer, composition should fit neatly into your schedule. It may even be possible to integrate the activities further, as shown in this example for my own experience.

In my early days as a music teacher in a secondary school, I met the poet and playwright Adrian Mitchell, and after some preliminary work together we wrote a musical for children: *Tamburlane the Mad Hen*. Having completed the work, I put on a performance at Blandford Junior High School in Dorset where I was teaching at the time and subsequently the full work was published.

Not only was the composition and production of this work good fun and good experience, it was beneficial to me in several other ways. Firstly, I was desperate not only to compose, but also to have my compositions heard. Secondly, it did my teaching career no harm. Thirdly, I earned a spot of extra money from the publishing of the book, and my compositional career took a step forward through the publication. Getting the first work published is always the hardest part.

Soon after the publication of this piece I was invited to talk to some trainee teachers about my experiences in putting on this play and other works I had written for schools. I said my piece, answered questions and afterwards we had a good conversation in the bar. During the chat it became clear that somehow the image that these teachers had of me was at variance with reality. They considered that by continuing to teach I was indulging a hobby; they assumed that (a) I was making a lot of money out of composition, and (b) I was naturally able to write what I liked and ensure subsequent publication and performance. Nothing I could say would dissuade them from this wholly erroneous view.

In fact, these trainee teachers *wanted* to believe that it was possible to become a 'composer' by writing, and having had performed and published, one musical. They needed this belief because for several of them the idea of spending the next 40 years in teaching was far removed from the ideal. What they were doing was preparing to earn money as music teachers while awaiting the 'break' that would lead them into full-time composition. Their problem centred entirely on their definition of a composer – to them a composer was not simply one who writes music, but rather one who has music published. So they labelled me 'composer' and expected me to conform to their image – someone involved in full-time composition, with no need of any other work.

In fact, I found it exceptionally hard to get my next work published, although I continued to work part time as a composer and have my works performed through my association with, among others, the Scratch Orchestra – an *avant garde* ensemble run by the late Cornelius Cardew. Later I was employed as a composer-teacher with the Cockpit Theatre and Arts Workshop in London for whom I worked for four years, but still publication came only slowly. Although I never made it as a professional composer, I did write some music during this period of which I remain quite proud. I certainly enjoyed myself a good deal and it also prepared the way for my subsequent career.

The early publication of *Tamburlane* even helped me to beat off heavy competition to get my post with the Cockpit Theatre. I recall sitting with the five other short-listed candidates in the theatre coffee bar awaiting the start of the individual interviews, having already been shown around the complex. One of the other interviewees came from a teaching background like myself, and quite naturally we started to exchange experiences. After a few minutes I discovered that she knew my name very well, as the last production she had put on was none other than *Tamburlane the Mad Hen*. Both our application forms for the job contained some details about performances; mine contained the additional fact that I had written the work.

With my continuing lack of progress as a professional composer, I gradually found alternative outlets for my creative efforts, away from composition, and I eventually recognized that I wasn't ever going to take composition beyond the stage of part-time work plus the occasional performance and publication.

To what can my failure to establish myself as a composer be ascribed? Firstly, the fact that I did employ alternative outlets – initially in writing arrangements of pop songs for the classroom. Secondly, to a lack of dedication; I did not make composition the centre of my life, but rather a major hobby. (I was at the time also studying science at the Open University, which, itself, took up quite a few hours each week.)

Finally, I failed through a lack of classical compositional training. If you are serious about becoming a composer you need training – even if you are planning to break every compositional rule in the book, you need to know what those rules are before you start. What's more, a good teacher will probably be in touch with others who can help in the development of your career – keeping you in touch with competitions and opportunities for putting work forward to the BBC and so forth. If you take lessons at a music college, or study privately with a teacher who is based at a college, then you may well be able to gain access to groups of performers who might be willing to take your work on. Indeed, you may find the opportunity of writing for particular groups, knowing that one or more performances will result. However it happens, it is worth recording each performance so that you have something to play to the next person who is interested in your work, but do remember to gain the permission of each performer concerned.

Certainly you should enter competitions, and although it is true that the more you enter the more experience you get, as with performance competitions, it is rarely worth entering something in which you have no chance at all of getting a prize. It must be added that even the winning of a competition is no guarantee of continuing success. But it can help, especially since some competitions do offer, as part of the prize, both the performance of the winning piece and the commissioning of a further piece which is also guaranteed a performance.

The *British Music Yearbook* lists some twenty competitions of various types for composers. From such competition entries one can build further, working with players from local groups, which itself may lead to working with performers under the sponsorship of the regional arts association.

Likewise, festivals should not be ignored, nor should the vast array of recreational courses which are advertised in *Musical Times*, *Classical Music* and *Music Teacher* in the early months of each year. A list also appears in *British Music Education Yearbook*. Apart from the chance to develop a piece during such a course, and the tuition that is available, it is always possible to strike up friendships which can be of lasting value as one looks for performers who will take on particular works.

In an ideal world one should always aim to write music upon commission and for players one knows. To write otherwise – which basically means to write what *you* want without any idea of how it will ever get to be performed – may give one a feeling of perpetuating the tradition of the artist-in-garret, but it does little else. No one is going to hop out of the wardrobe and say, 'I have been watching, you are a genius, I will have an orchestra perform your work tomorrow.'

Consider, on the other hand, the following. You write a piece for a group of friends you met at a summer school. One of the performers takes a score to another course, where he meets an arts administrator who is interested in arranging a performance of new pieces by previously unheard composers in a concert in a few months' time. The concert takes place and a recording is made. Not much money comes the way of the composer and the performers for this – in fact, photocopy fees and travelling expenses mean the composer is by now out of pocket, but the tape is made – a performance has taken place. Next the tape is sent to the local radio station, which agrees to make a new recording of the piece for broadcast on the monthly creative arts show. A little more money comes in, but the audience is tiny – the programme is a token gesture to contemporary arts and is put out at 9 p.m. on a Wednesday.

However, the composer makes a stereo cassette recording of the programme and sends it to a producer for the BBC region and to the music controller at Radio 3. After a while the BBC listening panel suggest that the work would be broadcast if the composer could arrange a new performance. With his many contacts the composer now gets his original team of performers together and, armed with his promise from the BBC, goes back to the arts administrator who happily arranges to promote the concert with the BBC outside broadcast unit present.

The point is simple – via this route of chance meetings and opportunities seized, the options for a hardworking composer are still not great but they are increased. But don't forget – all this while the composer is not earning money, so he has to have another job or be condemned to the dole.

Throughout all this activity the composer may wonder how best to arrange to have his work published. There is virtually no chance of getting an unknown, rarely performed work into print through an established publisher, so it may be better to turn to self-publishing. This is normally far less grand an enterprise than it sounds. At its simplest, you start by inventing a company name (no need to register it, but avoid the names of famous enterprises and, especially, avoid duplicating the names of firms already operating as record companies or music publishers). Then write to the Performing Right Society (known throughout the industry as PRS), telling them the firm's name and address, and giving a full list of works with the name of the composer. Next get in touch with the *Music Week Directory* and the *British Music Yearbook*, who will give your company a free listing under music publishers.

You now exist as a music publisher, and all you need is the music. Copy out your music *very neatly*. Now type the title and name and address of your publishing company, along with the copyright information, on a cover page and you have your master copy. If anyone wants a copy, photocopy it and sell it at an agreed price.

Finally in this section we turn to the question of writing music for television, films and broadcast commercials, known as jingles. In these areas, perhaps more than anywhere else, composition becomes a question of knowing the right people. All film and television work is done at speed, and producers need to be assured that the composer assigned to the task is not only going to complete in time, but also that the quality of his work is going to be so high that there will never be a question of turning anything down.

Contracts can often be made while still at college, perhaps through working on a film made by fellow students as part of a visual arts course. You may get to know people through other work you undertake, especially via arts centres and the like. And, of course, once you have broken through you will become known as the man or woman who wrote the music for such and such a film. So long as that is a positive statement to make about you, you will be on your way.

5
Songwriting

Many people feel they have the ability to write the sort of pop songs that could become hits. In reality very few people succeed, although this lack of success is often related as much to a lack of knowledge of how the songwriting business works rather than to the music industry's unwillingness to listen to new material.

It is no good writing a song that sounds exactly like someone else's hits. In addition to following the usual pop or rock formulas, all successful new songs have something a little different or unusual about them. If your songs do not have that 'extra something' or if they do but it sounds like someone else's 'extra something', you will probably find song selling hard going. If your song could just as well have been written by a proven writer, why should anyone choose to take a risk on the same sort of song from an unknown?

In short, your attitude as a would-be songwriter should not be, 'I can write something like that.' Nor should it be, 'I can write better than that.' Instead it should be the more complex, 'I can write a song which is just as commercially entertaining as that, but which includes an ingredient not heard before in pop music, an ingredient which the fans will love and which will mark the song out as mine and mine alone.'

How to start as a songwriter

Firstly, if you only write music, or only write lyrics, you need a partner. You can advertise for a songwriting partner in magazines such as *Melody Maker* or *New Musical Express*. Don't be tempted to pay an agency to write music to your lyrics. Such companies invariably churn out tunes by the hundred and typically make very little effort to get such songs accepted commercially, whatever their promises. They are, in short, simply after your fee for setting your lyrics to music which they use over and over again.

The most beneficial way of working, if you only write music or lyrics, is to team up with someone else and for both of you to work together in a rock group which will perform some of your pieces. There is nothing better than actually hearing your work performed over and over again to help you get the work into its true perspective.

Secondly, write as many songs as possible. Play and sing them to yourself and to others. Listen carefully to all opinions expressed. Consider: if *you* heard the song for the first time on the radio while you were doing the washing up, feeding the cat, having breakfast, or driving home from work, would it really interrupt your flow of thought? Would it make you want to hear the song again? Would it make you want to buy the record?

Next choose three or four songs from your repertoire and arrange for recordings to be made of these songs. If you are working with a group these recordings can be made by the group, and can be part of the group's attempt to get a recording contract. If you do not work with a group you can make a recording yourself or with one or two friends.

The quality of the recording

At this stage you can record the songs at home with simple guitar accompaniment, use a portable four-track studio, or hire a professional studio. Three well-rehearsed songs played by a competent rock band can be recorded and mixed in about three hours of studio time. For goodness sake, don't try to write or arrange the songs in the studio – these things can be done in your normal rehearsal room.

Studio time costs money and the impoverished songwriter will be pleased to learn that a four-track recording is not essential; a brilliant song presented via a recording of the songwriter singing accompanied only by an acoustic guitar will be accepted. The interesting (but not quite brilliant) song still stands a chance of success, but its chances will be enhanced through submitting a recording made by a group on decent equipment.

When deciding how to proceed it is certainly worth bearing in mind that many schools now own their own portable studios, and young songwriters may well be able to enlist the help of the local school's music department, especially if there is some connection between the songwriter and the school. If your memory of a school music department is one in which pop and rock music had no place, do remember that in recent years such things have changed, largely through the advent of the composition and performance requirements of the GCSE exam.

Having recorded the songs, you should send the tape either to an appropriate record company or a music publishing house.

The golden rules for submitting songs

● Always address the tape to the Artists and Repertoire Manager.
● Never send an original tape; only send a copy. Cassettes are easy to handle and cheaper to post than reel-to-reel tapes, and since high quality is not vital at this stage, cassettes are fully acceptable.

● Only send a tape or cassette to a company that deals in the type of music you are writing. Don't send reggae music to a company that only deals in top twenty pop, for instance.

● If you are unsure which publishers take your sort of music, look at the labels of records which are similar in style to your music, and there you will find the name of the publisher. Addresses of publishers can be obtained from *Kemps*, the *Music Week Directory* and the *British Music Yearbook*.

● Always send a clearly typed copy of the lyrics with the tape. Include very brief notes on the sort of arrangement you think is suitable for your song.

The direct approach: visiting a publisher

Approaching potential publishers in person can be very rewarding, for it helps to mark your material out from everyone else's in the publisher's view. It also means that even if the publisher doesn't like your material he may take a moment to say why and to give the odd comment on how you might go about improving your work. Above all, when someone who knows a little about such things takes time to make comments on your work, obey the ultimate golden rule: *listen, don't defend.*

Defending creative work is a trap we all fall into from time to time. You are naturally proud of your creative achievements. If someone says the ending of a song is all wrong, you feel the need to justify your approach.

Train yourself out of this defensive habit. Listen carefully; you never know, the person you are speaking to may be right, especially if he or she is in the music business and you are not.

This does not mean that you should accept each and every comment made on your music, but rather that you should remember that the person speaking to you may be saying, 'Make this change and you could have a publishable song.' Ask yourself: 'Am I so proud that I cannot accept that piece of advice?'

Copyright

Many songwriters worry about copyright, although this is, in fact, a very straightforward matter. If you write out something which is your original work, sign and date it and add the international copyright symbol (the letter c in a circle) with the year following it, you then own the copyright of that item. If you don't actually write the music out, you can record it and write the title, your name, the copyright symbol and year on the tape box and that will do. The copyright remains with you until your death, and then passes on to whom ever you nominate for the next 50 years. After that the music is out of copyright, and anyone can use it without payment.

If you want to be extra careful about copyright, you can put a copy of your song in a Post Office registered envelope, post it to yourself and keep it unopened with the date receipt. The receipt carries a number which is also on the parcel and this will prove that the parcel was posted to you on a specific date – proof that you had the song before anyone else.

Sadly, some would-be writers appear to be better at protecting their copyright than at writing songs, and there is a strong argument that suggests that such precautions are rarely necessary and can divert you from the real task of writing. There are a few copyright infringement cases each year involving songs, but they represent only a fraction of 1 per cent of the songs published. No reputable publisher is going to be involved in any deliberate attempt to try to defraud you of your copyright since there is no real advantage to him in doing this. The amount of royalty you will be paid per song is not great. Only if your song becomes a hit will the royalties be large, but then so will the publisher's take. If you can write one hit the chances are you can write two, but you are unlikely to work a second time with the same publisher if you feel he is taking you for a ride. It is therefore as much in the publisher's interests to be honest with you as it is in your interests to avoid stealing someone else's song. Try to choose a publisher who has already published a number of songs of the type you write – at least that will reduce the chances of being ripped off.

The role of the publisher

Occasionally some pop groups, who are actively writing and performing their own material, are approached by music publishers offering them a contract. This document, they may be assured by everyone who sees it, is perfectly straightforward and legitimate, so they sign. No money changes hands at this stage, but there is obviously hope of some to come, otherwise why bother with a contract?

Throughout the period of a contract publishers own the rights to publish the sheet music of the songs assigned over to them. Songs are not printed unless they become top forty hits or are from a top-selling album. Thus no record deal will mean no action, no sales and, of course, no money.

If a song is recorded the publisher will oversee the collection of all money due to the songwriter from all sources. The writer should receive not less than 10 per cent of the selling price of every copy of the sheet music of his song sold. This means that if the sheet music retails at £1.00 the songwriter gets 10p. The songwriter will get a percentage from overseas sales of the sheet music of the song. Deals will vary from country to country, but the writer should expect to get about half the total money the publisher makes from music sales outside the UK (although quite separate arrangements may be made with regards to the USA because of the size of the American market).

Also there will be some income from other printed uses of the song; something for lyrics only, something for inclusion in songbooks. The publisher may himself want to offset printing costs against these and other incomes, so look out for any clauses which deduct print costs from royalties. All in all, sales of sheet music are often low, and you should not expect to make more than a few hundred pounds from this source, unless you write a top ten hit.

The major source of income for the pop songwriter is the money paid by record companies for use of your copyright material. You should expect to get 6.25 per cent of the actual selling price of the record. So assuming a round sum of £1.15 for a single (of which you wrote both sides), deducting VAT at 1988 rates will give £1.00, of which you will get 6.25 per cent or just over 6p per record.

6
Management, agencies, roadies and discos

As you will have noticed, the terms 'manager' and 'agent' vary in their meaning somewhat as one moves from the world of pop to the classics. Often one finds in pop that an individual group will have a manager, who will turn to an agent when booking a tour. In the world of the classics, many performers are soloists booked into individual events; for such people there tend to be agents, each handling a wide range of artists. To make it more confusing, classical agents are sometimes referred to under the term 'management'. Someone looking for an agent may be said to be 'approaching management'.

What all these agents and managers have in common is the desire to book musicians into performances that will help the career of the musicians involved and make some money, both for the musicians and the management.

To look at this in more detail consider a recently formed pop group. Pop groups, in their early days if not later, seek out bookings playing at dances and concerts. To get such bookings they will need:

● publicity.
● someone to organize their transport and finances.
● someone to guide them when they come to sign a record contract, publishing contract and the like.

With a new group one person may take on many or all of these jobs. A friend with a van may be willing to drive the group and their equipment to dances and will, undoubtedly, help to load and unload equipment.

If this van-driving friend is able to help to get bookings, so much the better, and in return the group, being an honest and reasonable bunch of people, will pay him or her part of their earnings. If he is really pulling his weight then a group of five, who are currently taking 20 per cent of the earnings each, may well agree to split everything six ways, reducing the percentage but increasing their earnings over all through getting better paying bookings.

Later the van-driving manager may become the road manager, organizing hotels, travel, transport, food and the like for the group on the road. His percentage cut may well go down as he gives up the booking part of his job, but, again, if all is well his earnings will rise as the group becomes an ever-greater success. He will control a team of humpers and carriers, and may even organize a range of minders to ensure that the group is not endlessly hassled by fans.

63

Alternatively, our friendly helper might decide that he or she has had enough of living on the road and may wish to go into desk management. This could include making sure that the press know where and when the group is playing, sorting out the fine details of the record contract, liaising with a booking agent for a tour and so on.

If you wish to enter pop management you will probably begin either via contacts made at college or by going to clubs which regularly feature live music (you will know them already) so that when you find a group that you think has potential, you can offer to get them more bookings. It is indeed surprising just how many social secretaries from colleges and universities move into management in this way, retaining the knowledge of how the college booking system works.

If you don't know any member of the group that you are about to approach then there are three distinct ways in which they might react when you turn up backstage offering to get some bookings.

1. On the one hand the group might be suspicious, thinking that you are a rip-off merchant out to make money out of them.

2. Alternatively, they may misinterpret your suggestions and imagine that you are a big-time agent and that by stringing along with you they are now only one step away from stardom.

3. They may understand that you are fairly new in the business just like them, but that you can devote time, which they can't afford, to getting bookings.

Possibilities 1 and 2 both involve misunderstandings which can cause you problems. In case 1 you need to allay the group's fears. In the second case you need to keep the group's feet on the ground, for if they do continue to see you as a miracle worker they will soon be disillusioned when you initially supply more bookings of the type that they are already getting. It is amazing how quickly one member of a group can turn against a manager and either accuse him or her of taking money for nothing or of causing a lack of progress in the group's fortunes.

Much will depend on your demeanour, your personality, your style. One good idea is to stress that you will only take a percentage of the bookings that you actually get and won't receive anything if you don't succeed in finding them new work. Unfortunately, problems arise where you try to get a group booked once more into a place they played three months previously. Is this really new work or not? Is a commission payable?

The manager–group relationship should be a partnership based on trust. If the group remain hostile, it is better to forget it, as in this line of business there must be an element of trust and good will between the group and manager to begin with. Whatever work you get for such a band, there will be members of the group who will insist that they could do just as well without you. Be patient, remember you are dealing with people, and this is the line of work *you* have chosen. No one is forcing you to work with difficult, temperamental, highly strung, underpaid, overtired would-be superstars.

In approaching musicians in this way (as opposed to working with a group with whom you are already friends) you should be clear just how much you are offering to do for the group. For example, many groups have financial problems from the very start of their careers. Do you see it as part of your responsibility to try to sort out their financial situation, rationalizing debts and so on, or should you be spending your time chatting to your good friends on the college circuit, at local radio stations and so on, preparing for future bookings and publicity?

Having made your approach and set out your offer you now have to go about getting the promised new bookings. Here you should organize the biography – see page 31. You then take it to the various clubs in your area that you think would be suitable venues for the band.

You will appreciate at once that you can't go into this sort of work blind. Not only must you have a feel for what music is in demand and which musicians have real potential, you must also know who is booking in what sort of band in those clubs. You probably will know this because your interest in music is such that you are a regular visitor to the local clubs. If you are not, and you really don't fancy doing the research, then you shouldn't be thinking of this line of work.

From here on managers become involved in promotional activities for the band, which can include anything from having them photographed with a beauty queen to circulating or squashing a rumour that they were caught doing unthinkable things in the car park after the show. Which approach is chosen depends on the image the group wishes to present. Of course, publicity of this sort cannot sell records; it is still of primary importance that the band plays and is seen and heard playing.

When the group is ready, the manager should make sure that as many influential people as possible within the music industry are invited to selected concerts or dances. Getting newspaper critics and record company talent spotters to gigs is a hard task. The number of people who turn up to such events at his invitation, and the number he remains on speaking terms with as the months go by, is a fairly accurate indicator of how well a manager is doing.

Introducing Barry Tomes

Once started, agency and management work tend to develop their own momentum which leads the agent or manager into new fields through chance meetings and contacts. Barry Tomes, who owns the Birmingham based BT Management, told me of his own experience:

'After ten years as a tour manager working for all types of artists on gigs abroad and at home, I came across a young lady called Norma Lewis when I took on an American tour in 1985. At once I knew it was time to make the big step into artist management, so I dropped all pending tours.

'We have had success with Norma in many countries and, following her decision to take a year off to have a baby, we decided to expand into a full-sized management agency – we now book over 200 acts.

'After this amount of time in the business I now know for certain that the very next 'phone call can completely change your plans for a year – or even a lifetime.'

BT Management now not only books pop musicians, it also handles Radio 1 disc jockeys and even a few strippers. For the manager or agent in the classical sphere the work may appear more refined, but is essentially the same round of finding musicians, assessing bookings and holding the artist's hand. There is, however, one word of warning that needs to be added. If you are finding work for individual musicians (even if you do not end up paying them yourself but merely supply them as musicians or a group of musicians to a third party), you are technically operating as an employment agency, and under the Employment Agencies Act 1973 you must have a licence. Licences do take some time to obtain – four or five months is not unknown – and are expensive – upwards of £150 per year. The fine for operating without a licence can be in the order of £2,000. For more details contact your nearest Department of Employment and ask for the address of your local Employment Agency Licensing Office.

Roadies

In passing, mention has already been made of the men who are responsible for loading and unloading vans, erecting stage equipment and taking it down again, and sometimes driving the van as well. The job requires a strong constitution, as the roadie works all hours, catches up on sleep whenever and wherever possible and lives on whatever food happens to be available.

By way of illustration, if a band is due to play a show at 8 p.m., the roadies will be unloading and setting up from at least 5 p.m. At 11 p.m. they will start loading up again until perhaps 3 a.m. when they are theoretically free to get back to wherever they are staying for the night. However, it may well be that in order to get set up for the next gig on time the van must be driven away at once; the roadies will be expected to sleep, probably without having eaten, in the van. The van arrives at 3 p.m. the following afternoon, unloading starts again at 5 p.m. and so it goes for the duration of the tour.

A helpful list of trucking companies specializing in working for touring bands appears in *Kemps Yearbook*. Most people get into road work by starting with a local band or two, then buying their own van and hiring it out. It is also possible to build up work by contacting local band managers.

Promoting discos, concerts and artists

To run a disco, you must either work with your own mobile equipment or at a club. It can be difficult to find a club with its own disco equipment, but adverts do appear in the papers from time to time. You might even be lucky and find that the DJ at a club you know is about to leave and may be willing to recommend you to the owner as a possible replacement.

Equipment for a mobile disco consists of two turntables, a microphone, an amplifier and a pair of heavy-duty speakers. Almost all mobile discos now have a light show as well, and many also have a cassette or cartridge input for jingles. All such equipment is advertised regularly in the weekly music press. It may be worth while using second-hand equipment while you are starting up your business and then selling it to buy new equipment once you have found you can make a living at it.

You will also need suitable transport to get you to and from your bookings. You may hire or borrow a van, but whatever you do, make sure it is totally reliable and theft-proof, for once you get a reputation for not turning up on time (or turning up without your equipment) you will lose all chances of further bookings. To get bookings, you can either advertise in the local papers or get in direct contact with the owners of halls used for dances. You can even consider booking your own hall, selling the tickets yourself, employing bouncers and getting someone to run the bar. There are legal complications here, as you cannot simply set up a bar and begin to sell drinks – you need a licence from a magistrates' court – ask advice from a local publican or your local council. But don't try it until you are sure you understand how other people do it.

All discos need an up-to-date selection of records plus a number of oldies. Decide from the very start if you are going to specialize in soul, reggae, rock, top forty, hits from the 1950s and 1960s, etc. You can't cover everything, so consider what sort of audience you are likely to get and make it clear what music you offer in your adverts.

All major record companies have mailing lists of disco operators to whom they send their new releases, and to get on such a list you convince the company that you are operating your disco frequently enough to a large enough number of people for it to be worth their while giving you free copies. Approach the promotions departments of relevant record companies, either by 'phone or by letter. In writing, always use your disco's letterhead, and if you haven't got any, find a printer and get a few hundred run off with your trading name, the business address and 'phone number, and your own name. Be prepared to write if 'phoning doesn't work and vice versa, and don't be put off too quickly. Getting on mailing lists can take months of plugging away at the companies, and even then you will have to assure everyone that you are running your disco at least five nights a week.

7

Promotion as a profession

In theory anyone can put on a concert; you don't need a licence (unless, as stated on page 66, you are acting as an employment agency), and neither do you need to be a member of some large organization.

However, like all good theories this one has problems. You will need to show various people (such as the management of the hall or auditorium you wish to use) that you have the financial wherewithal to see the matter through. In particular, concert hall owners will be most wary of anyone who appears to suggest that they will only be able to pay bills after they get the takings on the door.

Most people start their work in promotion by arranging concerts for a specific location (e.g. a college arena) or particular musicians (a band you manage, or a band you play in). In what follows I will assume, however, that nothing is arranged and that you are starting from scratch.

It makes sense to start with the location. Different locations are suitable for different types of occasion. Consider how many seats there are, is there a bar, what are the acoustics like, what sort of car parking is available, what sort of events are associated with the hall.

You will also need to think about such aspects of the hall as its curtains (do they move properly?), the size of the stage, the changing rooms (deluxe or barely adequate?), the piano (in tune?) and so on.

Having thought about the type of event you wish to arrange, you then think about the concert as a whole, combining the location's idiosyncrasies with the style of concert you wish to arrange, choosing an appropriate date and looking out for anything else that might be in competition with your project. In doing all this you will be making a realistic assessment of your potential audience.

Now we come to detailed practicalities. Can you move in all the equipment you need without taking doors off? Is it going to be warm enough? Should you issue specific lighting instructions? Are there enough power points in the right places? Will the musicians need refreshments? If so, where will they come from?

Only when all these questions, and many more like them, have been answered will you be able to start work on the next major part of the operation – the finances. You now know what sort of event you are going to run, and you should be able to make a realistic guess at how many people you are going to get. Such a guess can be aided by a knowledge of how many people normally turn up to this sort of event at this type of location.

At this stage beware of arguments which say, 'No one has ever done this sort of thing before' or 'We can get more than they did – our publicity will be better'. If no one has done it before, it may well be because everyone else realized long ago that the concept you are planning would not get an audience at all. And are you really sure that the publicity used elsewhere was that bad? Remember, in many cases it is simply impossible to drum up a decent sized audience no matter what you do. The enthusiasts will show up, of course, but there are rarely enough of them to make a show a viable proposition.

You must prepare a full budget forecast before you book either the location or the artists. Income will come from ticket sales, sponsorship, programme sales, the bar, advertising within the programme and the like. Expenditure will come from the hire of the hall, the hire of the musicians, printing, bar costs, advertising, indirect publicity (press releases and the like).

Don't forget to account for VAT if you are registered. (If you are not registered and the ensemble you hire is not registered, it may be worth while staying unregistered in order to avoid charging VAT on the tickets. However, if the musicians are registered, or if VAT has to be imposed on the tickets because they are deemed to be sold by the concert hall rather than by you, then it will probably be worth registering before you start the financial arrangements for the concert.)

If you are booking an orchestra you will probably be involved in paying a fixer's fee, plus fees and expenses in accordance with Musicians' Union rules. Rock groups may simply have a set fee for the evening's work, although these may be subject to negotiation. With orchestral musicians you may also find yourself involved in special arrangements for overnight stays, late taxis, etc. Again, with pop groups these matters are normally left to the band and its own management. Rock groups will probably turn up in the late afternoon, set up, rehearse and retire to the pub. A concert for soloists may require one or more full rehearsals.

From here on you move into the world of publicity, and most concerts that fail fail here. Advertisements can bring in an astonishingly low response in advance ticket sales, and without advance sales you can never be sure how well things will go on the night. Public relations can help – a short interview on a local radio station and in the press can work wonders, but you must give the media a story to hang on to. Maybe there is a story in this being your first ever concert. Maybe the music is unusual. Possibly there is a strong local connection. Somewhere there must be more than the fact that 'A concert will be held at the Gas Works Road Memorial Hall on 12

April, and I think you ought to interview me about it.'

Naturally, you will want to sell as many tickets as possible, but there is also the need to give away some free tickets. The band may require some for friends, and the sponsor definitely will. The media should be sent tickets, as should anyone else who you think might turn up and could do you a good turn in the future.

From what has been said, you should realize that very few people will have the nerve to go straight into this type of work without some experience. Indeed, the information given here is still only a part of what you must do to ensure everything goes without a hitch. No mention has been made of the copyright fees which you will need to pay to the Performing Right Society, nor of the charges for hiring music for an orchestra, nor of 101 other things that the promoter must either see to or delegate. If you have started through booking music at college, all well and good, if not, make sure you start with a very small affair, and get in as many people as possible to help you. You can learn from your mistakes just as long as your mistakes do not bankrupt you in the process.

8
Musical work in radio and television

The BBC

One of the biggest employers of musicians outside the record companies is the BBC. BBC Television has a small number of music producers in its Music Programmes Department. Applicants for vacancies in the field must prove not only that they are musically qualified but also that they have visual imagination and some knowledge of cameras and film-making. This means that most of these producers have been trained at a university or music college, and so have traditional backgrounds in classical music. However, this need not always be the case.

The BBC normally only takes into employment as performing musicians those with professional musical qualifications, training and work experience. There are two types of opportunity: performing as a soloist or member of an orchestra and working on the staff of the Music Division in London or in a national or regional production centre. Soloists must have a high standard of accomplishment, and are never taken on on a full-time basis. Applications are handled by the BBC's Music Booking Manager, who holds auditions, as do the heads of music in other centres. Vacancies for orchestral players and choral singers are advertised in *The Listener* and other appropriate periodicals. In most cases only experienced players and singers can be accepted, although some are accepted straight from college. In London and also in non-metropolitan centres, part-time groups of singers and musicians are also selected from semi-professional local talent on an *ad hoc* basis.

Within the BBC music producers are responsible for devising, building, producing and supervising programmes; appraising standards of performance in studios, concert halls and auditions; working in close contact with artists and orchestras; keeping abreast of trends and developments in international, national and local music-making; maintaining good relations with the music profession, and contributing generally to the maintenance of high standards in broadcast music. Performance ability is not required, but a wide-ranging knowledge of music is essential and this may well have been derived through previous performance experience. In addition, the producer requires good professional qualifications, experience of organizing and promoting music, musical judgement, critical capacity, wide knowledge of repertoire and artists, ability to work to a plan and make management decisions, tact in dealing with musicians and imagination.

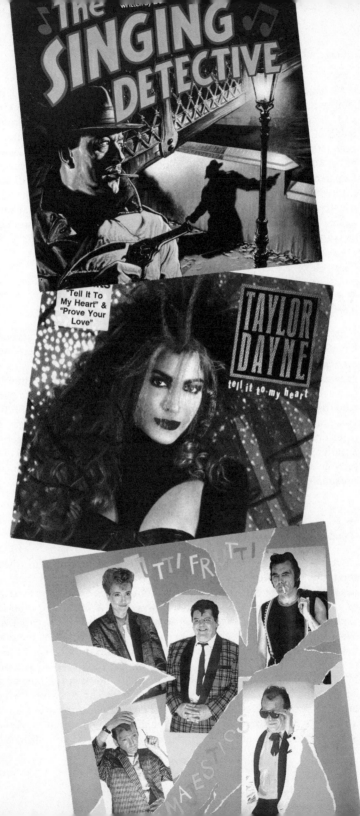

Management vacancies exist in the Orchestral Management Division, whose work includes the booking of deputy players and extras and day-to-day contact with the musicians. A good working knowledge of music is necessary, plus the ability to read a score and to understand the practical implications of assembling players. Details of all such vacancies can be obtained from the BBC Appointments Department. BBC jobs are also advertised in *The Listener*. Those interested in more popular music should be aware that such musicians are given contracts to perform on certain shows at rates agreed with the Musicians' Union. They are selected by the producer as being suitable for a particular show and are usually brought to the attention of the producer by their agents.

The ITV stations

Some, though not all, of the independent TV stations have their own heads of music, but none of them run their own orchestras. However, some do from time to time offer contracts to musical ensembles or support existing groups. More commonly, however, musicians in ensembles or groups are employed on a part-time basis or for a series of events, and such developments are often covered in *Broadcast* magazine. Musicians engaged to provide an interlude within a show, for example, are booked via their agents. Smaller TV stations often employ a musician as consultant, who may provide some musical items himself and arrange to bring in outside musicians as needed.

The ILR radio stations

Independent local radio stations do not normally have the funds to employ full-time musicians. However, some of them do occasionally offer contracts to musical ensembles or support existing groups. As with the ITV stations, however, it is more common for them to employ musicians in ensembles or groups on a part-time basis for an event or series of events. It is part of the agreement between the ILR stations and the Musicians' Union that a percentage of each station's revenue must be spent on live music, so all stations have the obligation to spend money on music, not just the larger and better-known ones. In view of this fact it might be worth while bringing your abilities, or those of your ensemble, to the attention of a station's programme controller through a demonstration tape. It is also worth noting that some professional musicians do move into full-

or part-time work with the ILR stations in a variety of capacities. One example is Ed Welch, the well-known composer and arranger who has written the music for a wide range of films and been associated with the music of many of Spike Milligan's television and stage works. He has made a place for himself on radio introducing programmes of film music, using his expert knowledge to give extra interest to the pieces he plays. He has further developed his media work and became musical consultant for TSW, the commercial television station for south-west England.

However, you need not be an established composer in order to broadcast on radio as a disc jockey! Approach the stations by preparing a short tape of yourself introducing discs (you need not actually play the pieces you introduce in their entirety, simply play a few bars, fade out and then fade in with a few closing bars and begin your next introduction). Send this to the programme controller of the station, along with a covering letter explaining your background and knowledge of the subject. Show that you have an original contribution to make, perhaps through a detailed knowledge of one type of music plus a familiarity with the music scene locally and an ability to comment on forthcoming events.

9
Working in a recording studio

There are a number of different staff positions within the recording studio, including producers, recording engineers (or just engineers), maintenance engineers, cutting engineers, administrators, tape operators and those euphemistically known as studio assistants but also called 'tea boys' and 'gofers' (because they are continually being told to go for this and go for that).

The studio assistant

The studio assistant is the lowest paid person in the studio and does the most menial work. He (or occasionally she) will be expected to be there at all hours when the studio is in session, arranging things on short notice, getting drinks and cigarettes for recording artists, going out to get an urgently required spare from the local supplier, sweeping up and so on. But in the process of carrying out all these menial tasks, the assistant gradually learns the work of the studio and begins to see which area he or she is most interested in.

To get work as an assistant you should locate the studios in your area, 'phone or visit them and see if you strike lucky. Consider carefully what attributes you are offering: a small motorbike and a clean licence, adaptability, the talent for staying awake long hours and a serious interest in the techniques of recording can all help. Not only must you be able to sell yourself by reference to such strong points, but you have to be a little lucky, arriving at the studio just after an expansion or the loss of the previous assistant. Through this system, only those whose desire to work in a recording studio is genuine and enduring will get through, as they are the ones who will keep on trying.

The tape operator

Assistants get promoted to tape operators. Now they are more truly 'assisting' the studio engineer in that they load machines, watch dials, check that leads are connected and so on. As time goes by, the studio engineer may well ask the tape operator (familiarly known as tape op) to take control during some of the less important sessions, and after a trial period he may find himself in charge of sessions during periods when the engineer is on vacation or off sick. The better the tape operator responds to such opportunities, the more likely he is to gain further promotion.

Working in a studio you naturally get to know what is going on elsewhere in the recording industry, both by reading the trade papers and simply by listening and taking part in everyday conversation. You are in a prime position, therefore, to receive early news of promising openings in your company or others and your chances of advancement are quite good, especially if you are willing to move around the country. The next step up is to become either an engineer or a producer.

The studio engineer

The studio engineer's job is to make the recordings the client (the musicians and their producer) requires. He or she has to interpret statements such as, 'Can you make it a bit muddier but with more top?' and translate them into practical suggestions for moving the microphones, changing the way tracks are mixed and so on. Even if he feels that a good piece of music is being ruined by carrying out these requests, it is not normally the engineer's job to say so. However, as an engineer becomes known for the individual quality of his work, his sympathy with certain musical ideas and skill in translating them into recorded sound, particular recording groups may ask that he be the engineer assigned to their sessions. Even so, the engineer is still answerable to the producer.

The monthly publication *Studio Sound* carries some job adverts as well as adverts and articles concerning the latest developments in studio equipment.

The maintenance engineer

The maintenance engineer must have a high degree of technical knowledge about the studio equipment, the way it works and how to repair it when it goes wrong. He or she will be aware of suppliers' claims for the tens of thousands of pounds' worth of complex equipment that even the most basic studio must have today, and part of his job is to make sure that these claims are fulfilled completely. Studio time costs a lot of money, and if a studio breaks down because of a fault in some small component in a minor piece of equipment, then the cost in terms of lost work can be astronomical.

Unlike the studio engineer, the maintenance engineer does not move up through the ranks but tends to come to the job with a good degree in physics or electronics and some experience of small studios. Sometimes people with these qualifications will start in low-paid jobs as tape operators and move on to maintenance work, but equally often they start off with the small studios and then graduate upwards.

The cutting engineer

The cutting engineer is responsible for getting the sound from the mixed down tape onto the master disc from which all copies of the eventual record will be made. He or she may work for either a large studio or the record company. The route to this highly complex and technical job is often by way of the assistant/tape op/engineer path. In fact, many cutting engineers were originally good studio engineers who found that they had a greater love for the equipment than for the musicians, who can, after all, be far more temperamental and demanding.

The producer

The producer may also have worked his way up through the engineering route, or he may have been a successful musician with an interest in engineering. It is normally he who decides exactly how the music should sound on record; whether, for example, violins should be used, whether the fade-out ending will work, whether the piece would be improved by double-tracking the voices, or whether the piano should be heard throughout instead of just fading in on the second verse. The proof of the producer's judgement is satisfied recording artists and records that sell. Producers who achieve such results regularly become highly sought after and command huge fees or percentages of a record's income.

Producers and engineers have one thing in common – if they become very good at their jobs, they tend to leave the studios with which they have become associated in order to broaden their horizons and, by the way, their bank balances. For producers who have become very well known, this normally means freelancing, with artists and their managers approaching the producer and offering him excellent contracts to produce their next record. For an engineer who has become recognized in his own right, the next step is often to set up a studio which then becomes the only place where his particular combination of expertise and talent are available.

Administration

Lastly, there are the administrators. Administration hardly sounds as exciting or attractive as studio engineering, and yet the work is just as essential as the engineer's. The job of the administration team is to make sure that the studio is as fully booked as possible and that the money owed is paid on time. Booking bands into the studio means advertising and promotion, and, as the studio becomes better known, approaching bands that are preparing to record a new single or album. If studio administration fails to pull its weight then there will be insufficient work for the engineers and the company will cease trading. Studio administrators come from all walks of life. Some enter as secretaries, some as young qualified accountants and some from management. The ability to type or, better, operate a word processor, plus an understanding of basic accounting, are very helpful indeed.

Buster Gobsmack eats Filth

WE WANNA BE FAMOUS

10
Working for a record company

Most record companies are predominantly concerned with popular music; only about 12 per cent of all records produced are classical and so there are far fewer jobs in record companies for those with an interest in classical music than for those interested in pop. However, classically orientated jobs do exist with the multi-national and major specialist companies in such areas as classical record promotion and as general administrators with the smaller specialist labels. Administrators with a wide knowledge of music and good business sense should have a reasonable chance of finding a suitable place.

Jazz occupies an even smaller segment of the market, but if you are a jazz fan you will know which record companies to approach. Addresses are in the music yearbooks listed in the bibliography (p.112).

Even smaller is the number of companies specializing in early music and music from non-western cultures. But if you have ability and a specialist interest you have nothing to lose by putting yourself forward for consideration.

When writing to, or telephoning, the personnel office of a record company, do remember that there is no standard type of record company – each one is different. There are the majors at the top – themselves part of giant conglomerates which may have interests in car hire, video equipment, satellite television and a million other things. At the other extreme are the one- or two-person firms producing the music they believe in and seeing sales of just 1,000 copies of a disc good reason to open a bottle of champagne. In such a firm there is no such thing as a department – everyone does everything. In a major record company there will be a marketing manager, production department, sales director, sales manager and many more individuals in addition to those sections listed below.

Almost all companies producing more than half a dozen records a year ought to have the following departments.

Press and publicity

The work of the press office involves publicizing records and artists on tour and supplying reviewers with copies of records and background information, photos and the like. The press office will seek to make a major impact in the media with new pop artists and important new recordings by famous classical soloists. Part of this work involves ensuring that the musicians not only get good press coverage but the right sort of press coverage – for example, making sure that the musicians' work is written up in those publications most likely to be read by potential buyers of the records.

Many press officers join record companies from other jobs in writing such as music journalism, or from writing arts pages in non-music magazines and papers. The press officer needs to be able to communicate freely with journalists, so it is obviously to his or her advantage to have worked in journalism in the past. (More details on music journalism appear in Chapter 13.)

Promotions

The promotions department of a record company is similar to the press office, but specializes in getting records played on the radio. It normally deals with singles (which it may also supply to reviewers and even DJs in discos) rather than LPs, and in most cases deals with pop rather than classics (even though radio stations will want to have a number of classical LPs in their record libraries).

The artists and repertoire (A and R) department

As we have already seen, A and R is concerned with finding new artists and music for recording. A and R departments are small but powerful since they contain the people who decide just what gets onto record. The A and R manager has to ensure that new records are not only in accordance with the company's usual standards of artistic and technical excellence, but also in keeping with the style of music or 'image' of the particular label.

A and R departments are normally overwhelmed with offers of music, 90 per cent of which is rubbish. Such efforts usually contain no structure or musical awareness or even novelty value. Yet even after the rubbish has been sifted out there remains far more music than any single company can handle. Next comes the 'image' sifting, a process which involves looking for music which will fit in with the declared style of the record label. After this A and R departments will sort out music which the departmental staff do not personally like. This may seem very unfair – many a would-be musician or composer has been heard to cry, 'This is what the people want; it is irrelevant that you don't like it.' But the department has to work with anything that it takes on, and since there is more than enough music on offer it makes sense to work with music one likes.

The label manager

Each record label has several individuals, or even teams of individuals working on different aspects of the record label's output – A and R, publicity, promotions and so on. Each of these departments has its own interests, concerns and, indeed, its own budget. There will be co-operation of course, but there will also be tensions as one department blames problems and failures on another – A and R blaming a flop on bad publicity management, promotions blaming the failure to get radio plays on the poor selection procedure in A and R and so on. And always everyone will want more money in order to expand their department and, so they claim, do their job better, faster, etc., etc.

These conflicting feelings are balanced, and overall policy decisions made, by the label manager. Normally label managers have worked their way up from other aspects of the operation, having shown a solid combination of people-skills and administrative and financial ability. They may come in from outside the record industry but they always bring with them a lot of relevant experience.

11
Your own record company

Starting up your own record company is not nearly as difficult as it sounds, although you should read one of the innumerable books about setting up a business before getting involved.

The method is simple. You find a group that is playing at clubs or dances in your area, ask them to prepare an hour or so of material, and then hire an eight-track studio for a day or two to record it. Having mixed the recording and selected the best 40 minutes' worth, you pay a custom printing company to press 1,000 copies of the LP, while contracting with a label printer to design the centre label and a sleeve printer to work on the outer cover. (All the names of the companies you would need to deal with can be found in the Yellow Pages or the industry yearbooks. Alternatively, ask a rep for a small local company where it gets its pressing and so on done.) You then travel with the group to their dances and concerts and try to sell your 1,000 records. You should be able to sell these at well under the normal LP price and still make a profit, even after you have paid all the expenses and given the group, say, 8 per cent of the takings.

Apart from the profit to be made, one of the great advantages of running your own company is that you have artistic control over the type and quality of music that goes out. With your own company, if you feel that the major record companies are ignoring your type of music, all you have to do is launch the records yourself. Pricing is, in fact, one of the most difficult and crucial things you will be concerned with in running your own company. It is very easy to make basic errors at this stage and then find you have done all your work for nothing. For example, let us assume your own group has made an LP in a studio. The cost of the studio time was very low (say £250) because the engineer was a friend and let you have otherwise dead time at a give away rate. The cost of pressing 1,000 records, including printing the sleeves and labels, was £450. On this basis, you would appear to be producing 1,000 records for £700. Sell them at £1 each and it looks like you have £300 profit. In fact, this is not quite true. The £300 apparent profit has to be shared among all the people involved, and assuming that a total of ten people were involved equally in making the recording and each of them worked a total of 60 hours, they would each be receiving 50p an hour for their work, including you. And there is worse to come. If your records are to be sold to the general public at concerts, you may want to pay someone to do this. If you sell via specialist record shops, they will want a commission on each sale. And you still have to cover such ordinary running costs as 'phone calls, stationery, postage, transport and so on. And then you have to allow for the possibility that you may not sell all the records.

If your recordings are of songs written by yourself or your group, there are no formalities to be entered into. However, if someone then copies your record or songs, you may find it hard to prove your copyright. The answer is to register with the Mechanical Copyright Protection Society (MCPS). Certainly, if you record music composed by other people, you are obliged to deal with MCPS or one of the related organizations. People work hard to write, perform and record music, and they naturally expect to get paid for doing it. Thus their songs, arrangements and recordings are copyrighted. Not only is it not possible to record other people's work without paying for it, but you cannot hire a hall, set up a disco and charge people to hear you play records without paying the copyright owners for the right to do so.

These matters of copyright are handled by a set of limited companies which exist to collect the fees payable by law and protect the rights of those they represent. This means that payments can be made to a central organization without the individual having to locate and negotiate with the copyright owner himself. The main companies concerned with these matters are the Mechanical Copyright Protection Society, the Performing Right Society, and Phonographic Performance Ltd. The simple rule is, if you are intending to work with copyright material in any way, get in touch with these societies and request their free leaflets explaining various aspects of their work.

Recently, the government has done much to help with the development of small businesses. There is no point in listing all the government schemes here as they change with such rapidity, but some general points can be made. Firstly, contrary to popular belief, the high street banks are perfectly willing to lend money to small businesses as long as that loan can be guaranteed in some way. For example, if you wish to borrow £5,000 and you can raise a further £5,000 yourself, then, if you or your parents own a house, the value of that house can guarantee your overdraft. The way to approach a bank is with a comprehensive set of figures showing your expected outgoings and income over a three-year period.

Secondly, there is a government scheme which enables people who are out of work to continue to claim their dole money while setting up in business. Thirdly, when you do start you will need some staff, and there are schemes enabling you to take on unemployed school leavers at low rates of pay which the government then reimburses to you. Fourthly, in virtually all parts of the UK there are local groups which help with the setting up of small businesses. Information about them and the other schemes mentioned can be obtained from your local Small Business Information Centre.

Detailed information about finances cannot be given here, as this depends upon circumstances and can only come from a bank manager, finance company, accountant or the Inland Revenue. However, an important tax concession is available for anyone who is in full-time employment (or whose spouse is in full-time employment) and who is starting up a new business at the same time. Expenses incurred in setting up such a business (including everything from buying machinery to the cost of 'phone calls) can, for tax purposes, be offset against tax payable on any other income earned by yourself or your spouse. Thus, if you earn £8,000 a year as a car mechanic and start a business buying and selling second-hand records, you might find that you make a loss in the first year. However, you can apply many of your costs in setting up the record business against your income as a mechanic, which will reduce your level of taxation considerably. The local Inland Revenue office will help you with details, as will the excellent tax-saving guide published each March by *Which?* and available in most public libraries. The tax and personal finance columns in some Saturday and Sunday newspapers occasionally print interesting information in this area as well. However, it should be emphasized that unless you are very knowledgeable about finances you should employ an accountant. This is particularly important when the business gets going and you become involved in the intricacies of VAT. .

12
Making a living by selling records

Running a record shop

The main point to be made about running a record shop (or, indeed, any business) is that you should not set up your own business until you have worked for someone else and observed very closely how each aspect of the operation works. Selling records or tapes by mail order is a much less risky affair as one of the major expenses, the shop, is eliminated, and the whole thing can be done in your spare time.

The best way to set up a mail order business is to select and deal in a speciality (reggae, hard rock, etc.). You can then stock up with a small number of albums of specialist appeal and advertise in the appropriate magazines. Every time you get an order you add the customer's name and address to your mailing list so you can send him new record lists as they become available. Thus, a person who buys one record in response to your advertisement may later receive one of your lists and decide to buy two or three more, and so on. You can also buy and sell second-hand records in your chosen speciality. People answering your advert might want to sell you records which you could then re-sell at a profit. You can often pick up large lots of records very cheaply from local auctions or from advertisements in the trade papers and *Exchange and Mart*, although you must always keep an eye on the condition of the product you are being offered. Another source of second-hand records is open to you if you can offer to travel to the homes of people living in your area and make them a cash offer on the spot.

You will need to contact the record companies and wholesalers whose records you are interested in selling, to see what sort of a deal they can offer you. You will also need a space at home, perhaps a spare bedroom, where you can store your stock, a trading name and a bank account. In setting up a mail order business, you will also need to work with a printer to prepare your advertising literature. Check through the Yellow Pages for the names of local printers and request quotations so you can find who is offering the most competitive price for the kind of printing required.

Import/export work

This is an interesting and potentially profitable area of record and tape sales. There is, without doubt, a big demand in Europe for British rock music. In 1992 trade barriers are to be withdrawn across the EEC and this could become a most lucrative area. Get an agent, who speaks the language and will be able to negotiate at that end, working in the other country or countries. Also contact the Embassy and British trade delegation for the country you wish to export to. Addresses can be found in the London 'phone book. Explain what you want to do to a representative of the trade delegation and if they can't advise you they will certainly tell you who can.

Remember that cassettes and CDs are easier to transport around Europe than records. Also remember that if you build up an account in some countries it is often impossible to transfer the money back to your home country without paying heavy duties. One way to get around this is to leave some money for holidays in that country. Another is to arrange to import something from that country to the UK which can then be sold, so that you get your money back through trade. Beware of taxation. You may find that you are being asked to pay tax on your income in two countries. This can be overcome, but you will need an accountant to advise you and tell you which country you should pay tax in. There are tax advantages, too, including expense account trips in the country you are exporting to. See your accountant for details.

Most imported records cause no difficulty with regard to copyright clearance. However, some recordings from the USA do cause a problem, and if you are considering importing records you should check the position with MCPS as to possible payments due to the society.

Lending libraries

Lending out records and cassettes at a fee has been going on for some time, although the lending of CDs has only recently been gaining in popularity. You will, of course, need to purchase a wide range of records or tapes before you can start your library, and it might be worth while exploring the idea of a specialist library which you can advertise in specialist magazines. Normally, a registration fee is charged and the customers also pay for each record or tape borrowed. However, there are many variations on this format. The loan can be tied in with a second-hand mail order business in which each item is sold to the customer at the normal price and then bought back, if the customer so wishes, at a lower price. Alternatively, the customer can pay a fixed registration fee, borrow records and exchange them whenever he wishes.

13
Writing about music

There is a very large number of magazines that either deal exclusively with music or regularly carry information about it, and publishers show no sign of stemming the steady flow of books on music at all levels. Writing is equally as competitive a profession as performing or composing and it should be entered with whole-hearted commitment, not as a last resort when you find it impossible to get your preferred employment elsewhere.

Before you start writing make sure you have a very clear idea of what is required. It cannot be stressed too much that it is up to the writer to study his or her market. Time after time publishers receive manuscripts they cannot possibly publish, not because the writing is bad, but because they simply do not handle books or articles of that type, length, style, etc.

Would-be authors should consult a standard reference work detailing the UK publishers and the types of work they publish, such as *Writers' and Artists' Yearbook*, published by A & C Black. It gives the names and addresses of hundreds of UK book publishers, magazines and newspapers on all topics, as well as a lot of general advice to writers.

Music is a medium particularly difficult to translate into the written word. Learned analyses of form and style tend to be lost on the average reader, as do reviews which adopt a lyrical or metaphorical approach to the subject. In the world of pop music this problem has been overcome by concentrating largely on the personalities and personal lives of the stars, an approach which is seldom justified in writing about classical music, although, of course, great personalities do emerge from time to time. Another problem for the writer is that many specialist music magazines have such a small readership that payments for articles are often similarly minuscule and rarely cover the costs incurred in preparing the article. Some magazines concentrate on the politics of music, others develop an idiosyncratic style. Always take time to read what the editor is choosing to publish at present.

Mention must also be made of reviews. Reviewers often suffer poor payments, although they normally have the bonus of free records and concert tickets. Anyone trying his lot as a reviewer should remember that the reader has the choice of several thousand other record or concert reviews ... yet another review, to justify its existence, will need something to set it apart from the rest, and this is seldom achieved.

Don't aim too high to begin with. Try small-circulation local magazines, local papers and specialist monthlies and present them with a positive offer. Don't write saying, 'I'd like to write for you, please tell me what sort of things you want.' Submit a sample of your style, perhaps a review of a new record you've just bought or of a concert you've just seen. Alternatively, write a general article on the latest music trend or fashion (preferably one that has only just started and on which you can add a local angle), and mention that you are also interested in writing reviews.

Many people want to know how they can get review copies of records, how to get complimentary press tickets for concerts and how to arrange interviews with pop stars. For LP records, simply write or 'phone the record company's press office, mention the name of the publication you are writing for and request the record you require. However, since many people who are not journalists at all try to get free records in this way, record companies tend to be cautious and it may be a good idea to include a copy of a recent article with your request for records to show that it is legitimate. The same procedure applies for singles, but you should write or 'phone the promotions department.

To get concert tickets, you can approach the press office of the performer's record company or the company promoting the concert. Again, do send along a copy of your published writing so they know you are genuine. Interviews are generally easier to get, especially with lesser known stars touring the provinces. Again, get in touch with the record company's press office, tell them who you want to interview, where, when and for what paper, and if the date and place coincide with the tour schedule they should be able to arrange it. Obviously, you can't expect someone touring in the London area to come to Glasgow to meet you, but if he is playing a concert in Cardiff and you are willing to go to the hall to do the interview before a performance, everything should be all right. But do start trying to arrange things several weeks in advance.

Of course, many people do develop careers in either music or book publishing, and here once again determination and enthusiasm are needed before you can get anywhere near a full-time reasonably paid job. As always, refer to the standard reference works listed in the bibliography for sources of possible employment.

14
Music education

There are two separate branches of music education. On the one hand, there are those teachers and lecturers who, for the most part, work full time in a single establishment teaching groups of pupils or students – most typically the classroom music teacher working in a primary or secondary school. On the other hand, there are the teachers of individuals or small groups of pupils. These may travel from school to school, also undertaking some private work in an individual's home or their own home. Some work full time, teaching only from their own home.

The full-time school teacher

In order to teach class music in a state school you need to be a qualified teacher, which involves undertaking a course at degree level and a teacher-training course – a total of four years. You do not have to take a course in music to be able to teach music, nor do you have to be qualified to teach in private school, a college or a university. However, it is unusual (and may be considered odd by a prospective employer) for anyone who is not correctly qualified in the right subject to apply for a job as a music teacher or lecturer.

Primary school

Some primary schools (but by no means all) have specialist music teachers whose work will include taking classroom music lessons, teaching basic instruments in the classroom (recorder, electronic keyboards, etc.), running a choir and possibly an orchestra, and liaising with visiting teachers who are teaching specific instruments. At lunch time and after school there may be rehearsals for school plays and the like.

Some musicians prefer not to be exclusively involved in music at primary level and so take up posts as general classroom teachers, teaching a wide range of subjects, but also taking on some specialist music work usually for additional payments. Often such decisions come from the teacher's own personality: some want to work with the children's whole education, others need to work in music and nothing but music.

Secondary school

There are very few secondary schools in the UK that do not have their own music departments, which means having at least one (and possibly two or three) teachers who teach nothing but music to pupils aged perhaps eleven to sixteen or eighteen.

Here the work will involve taking general music lessons, teaching for exams such as GCSE and A level, and working after school in rehearsal with the orchestra and choir.

Music in school is an area of work which is often described as high in stress and sometimes modest in the level of satisfaction it brings, although this is not to say that there are not many, many people who enjoy teaching music very much indeed. Upon entering a school for the first time, full of enthusiasm and grand ambitions, the newly qualified music teacher may soon run up against a situation for which he or she has been at best inadequately prepared – the average group of 30 teenagers with a profound lack of interest in, if not positive hostility towards, music of the classical and romantic era. For many young people classical music is old-fashioned and alien, a symbol of the adult world (also, to an extent, an educated middle class one) which is clearly set against their music.

Even though young teachers enter the schools full of excitement about their subject and the prospect of communicating it to the young, it is unfortunately true that many can never overcome their pupils' prejudices. The reasons are complex and need not concern us here, save to point out one very basic conflict – music lessons, if they are to be *real* music lessons, will often make a bit of noise. The problem relates to under-resourcing of departments, and repeated attempts by administrators to treat music as a subject just like any other inevitably lead to conflict and argument. In fact, school music is obviously different from school history since it is often quite impossible for 30 untrained music students to perform music and learn from that performance all in one room (although the advent of microtechnology and the development of portable studios are lessening the problem to some extent).

Some schools do have excellent facilities, and, indeed, some schools are particularly known for their musical excellence and strong emphasis on music. This is particularly true in the private sector. Details of schools specializing in music can be found in the *British Music Education Yearbook*.

Further and higher education

Teachers in colleges of further education may, like their secondary school counterparts, be teaching GCSE and A-level music.

In colleges of higher education, polytechnics and universities they will probably be teaching towards degrees in music, and will be highly qualified themselves, with a research degree as well as a first degree. The same will not be true, however, of those people working in colleges of music (sometimes known as the conservatoires), where the majority are professional performers with no teaching qualifications.

Work in this field is normally advertised in the *Times Higher Education Supplement*. Many applicants advance their careers by being well known to those on appointment panels through performances and publications. It is virtually impossible to gain work lecturing in music in a college or university unless you have completed at least one or possibly two degrees in music. I say 'virtually' impossible, because there are exceptions – courses in jazz, pop, reggae and other ethnic musics are becoming increasingly popular at all levels, and although many academics exist with the right qualifications, colleges often require the services of musicians with practical experience of these types of music.

The part-time school teacher

A part-time music teacher may be part time at a particular school, but when the hours at each school are added together, along with hours of individual tuition at home, then the teacher may well be undertaking more hours than a full-time teacher based in one school.

Typically such a tutor (often known as a peripatetic tutor) will teach individual students, or very small groups, on a particular instrument or range of instruments. Each lesson might last half an hour and, in most cases, will be on instruments of the classical orchestra – violin, flute, oboe, clarinet, cello, etc. Many schools also offer private piano lessons, although these are not always available because of a shortage of instruments available within the school, and a shortage of music teachers nationally.

In addition, some schools offer special tuition for steel bands, for folk guitar, rock guitar, classical guitar, electronic keyboards and a range of other instruments. Much will depend on the level of demand, the enthusiasm of the head of music in the school and the availability of teachers.

Certainly in many parts of the country there is a great shortage of private music teachers, and most instrumental teachers could fill their schedules up time and again if they had a mind to (although it is worth bearing in mind that this is not always the case in major cities where university or conservatoire students aim to earn additional cash by offering lessons). The going rate for private tuition in piano or on an orchestral instrument is currently between £2 and £4 an hour more than the rate for tuition of any other school subject.

While schools may wish to be assured that a teacher is qualified, this is not always the case with individual parents who merely wish to secure the services of a tutor for a child at home. Indeed, when it comes to teaching pop, rock, jazz and ethnic techniques it is often not at all relevant to ask if a teacher is qualified.

There is no doubt that anyone who enjoys playing, who wants to supplement an income with a spot of teaching, and who is able to explain how to perform to someone of far less ability and experience than themselves, can earn a reasonable living, with an almost endless stream of clients waiting at the door. Such teaching activity can be carried on virtually round the clock, with schools requiring staff through the day, private pupils seeking evening lessons, private and local authority music centres operating on Saturdays, and more private pupils coming along on Sundays. And if that were not enough, there are also adult evening classes organized in every part of the country, where groups of students can be taught certain popular instruments, such as guitar, flute, electronic keyboard and the like. Indeed a tutorial agency which I helped set up found work for over 1,000 part-time tutors in all subjects throughout the UK, but constantly had a desperate shortage of teachers of all musical instruments.

How to find work

Posts in schools and colleges are advertised in such publications as the *Times Educational Supplement*, *Teachers' Weekly*, the *Guardian* newspaper (currently specializing in education on Tuesdays), etc. There is no point writing to schools looking for full-time work since if there is a vacancy you will find the job advertised. However, it may be worth contacting schools, especially private schools, for work as an instrumental tutor, since, as suggested above, there is such a shortage that some schools may have a waiting list of pupils.

If you wish to work as a private tutor you can consider advertising in the local paper and through the local music centre. The Local Music Education Guide in the *British Music Education Yearbook* is particularly helpful since it gives information on the way each county organizes its music education and what sort of work it undertakes. Virtually every local education authority has a local music centre where you may well be able to teach a number of students and put up notices signifying the fact that you are available. You should also consider joining the Incorporated Society of Musicians, which publishes a yearly register of professional private music teachers which is circulated to music shops, libraries, etc.

Music shops can also be of help. Most towns have a music shop selling classical records, orchestral instruments, exam music and the like, and they often have a notice board displaying details of teachers. The same applies to shops specializing in the sale of pianos. Other shops specialize in selling organs and electronic keyboards, and they often organize keyboard tuition, which is sometimes arranged as part of the sale of an instrument. If it is clear that you will tell your students to buy their music from that shop, they may well agree to putting a leaflet up advertising your whereabouts.

Local authorities, requiring instrumental staff to work in a variety of schools, often advertise in *Teachers' Weekly*, the *Times Educational Supplement* and the *Guardian*. London-based tutors in rock instruments and singing also tend to advertise in *Melody Maker*. Elsewhere local newspapers are used.

At this stage it is worth remembering the comments made previously; often in music it is impossible to earn a full-time living from the particular branch of music that especially attracts you and, therefore, if you are a good teacher private tuition is a very good way of supplementing your income while keeping you in the world of music.

Lastly a word about musical literacy. The classical-romantic approach to music is dominated by a theory of musical notation and, traditionally, music teachers teach pupils to read music written in that way as they teach them to play. However, pop, jazz, the *avant garde* and other types of music are not based on conventional notation, and it seems sad to me that many young people go through their musical careers without any knowledge of improvisation or any sense of playing by ear. Somehow the classical musician sees playing without music as less worthy than playing with it. It is not, and there is no reason why music education should ever make it so.

15
Arts administration

The job of an arts administrator is to balance the needs and desires of the artist with those of the public, satisfying both as nearly as possible. Ideally the administrator understands and is sympathetic to the artist's need to have work exposed to appropriate audiences and the audience's need to be entertained, stimulated, occasionally educated and seldom offended by public promotion of the arts. Whatever his sympathies, his work must be conducted within the guidelines laid down for his particular organization, whether it be a regional arts association, festival or competition committee or local authority. The ideal may not be realizable but the chances of getting it right are greatly enhanced if the arts administrator has been trained in some aspect of the arts himself and is, for example, a musician who also happens to have good organizational ability.

Because the field of arts administration is a very competitive one, it is common for administrators within the regional arts associations to have had some prior experience of the work before getting a full-time administrative job. Many gain this experience at college or university, helping with the organization of exhibitions and events. A music student will naturally gravitate towards events in his own field of interest, but although arts administrators are appointed to work within a particular area of the arts, it is no bad thing to expand your interests and organizing experience to include one or two events outside your immediate area of concern.

After college it may seem that the opportunity to organize events is lost but this need not be so. The keen potential administrator should have no trouble in marrying locations, performers and audiences into events which can be run, if not at a profit, then at least not at a loss for local organizations. Certainly, this sort of background would be a positive recommendation when applying for a post as an arts administrator. It should be pointed out, however, that some people who follow this route never arrive, perhaps they cannot get a job, or because of the timely realization that administration is not for them, or, alternatively, because they have been so successful that they decide to continue their promotional activities on a commercial basis.

Most regional arts associations state that it is personality rather than qualifications that matters when they appoint new people. They will certainly expect a knowledge of the field or fields concerned, but the candidate's temperament is very important.

Some colleges are now offering courses in arts administration and regional arts associations are naturally interested in recruiting people who have completed such courses. However, graduates without such training may be taken on as administrative assistants attached to specialist officers within the association. Outside of the regional arts associations, some arts administration is undertaken by the entertainment and recreation departments of local authorities, normally under the municipal entertainment manager. The work of such a department is obviously very varied indeed, comprising everything from conference centres to sports centres, outdoor art shows to carnivals. Unlike the regional arts associations, many local authorities recruit school leavers rather than graduates, although some graduates and college leavers may be recruited, especially where the local authority has created the post of arts officer to act in direct liaison with the local association and the arts council. Some training courses are run from time to time. For details contact your regional arts association. Advertisements for arts administrators often appear in the specialist creative and media employment section of the *Guardian* on Mondays.

16
Building and maintaining musical instruments

Virtually everyone who is involved in either building or maintaining musical instruments has undertaken a course of study directly related to that work. I say 'virtually everyone' with regret, for although it is, in my view, impossible to undertake this type of work without training, some people still do. There are cowboys in the trade offering all sorts of repair work without any background training – my advice is that they should be avoided, and that no one should try to enter this field without undergoing a proper course.

There is a growing demand for early instruments, and the making of these requires craftsmanship, research, invention and experiment. The world of electronics gives even more opportunities both within and outside music. Given that such a course is so closely linked with one particular area of employment, it is not surprising that many people do find that experience and help at college lead on to employment thereafter.

One of the leading establishments in training in this field is Newark Technical College in Nottinghamshire. It runs, for example, a two-year musical instrument electronics course for which the entry qualifications are three GCSEs or O levels. Courses of this nature investigate the circuits which form part of electronic musical instruments, and students become involved in the construction of component units of amplifiers, keyboards, MIDI interfaces, sound-to-light units, effects pedals and the like, as well as studying computer hardware and programming.

A different type of training comes with the piano-tuning maintenance and repairs course also run at Newark. Such a course not only teaches students to tune pianos but also to repair and restore them. With such courses high-level musical skills are often not required, and they may therefore be suitable for people with an interest in and feeling for music, plus a bias towards practical subjects, rather than the academic or performance-orientated musician.

Newark runs similar courses in both violin- and woodwind-making and repairing. In all cases mature students are welcome as well as students straight from school.

Another major centre of training is the London College of Furniture, which includes apprentice-based courses related to Youth Training Schemes as well as courses for adults and unemployed people, plus part-time and evening courses. Subjects on offer include musical instrument technology, piano-tuning, stringed-instrument-making, woodwind construction and repair, steel-pan-making and repair and Indian instrument-making and maintenance. Music instrument repair is also offered at Merton College in Surrey.

West Dean College in Sussex offers a three-year apprenticeship scheme in the making of stringed musical instruments, in which the apprentices make about fifteen plucked and bowed stringed musical instruments. These instruments are then sold and the proceeds used to support the apprentices during their third year at the college. As with most courses in this field, there are no formal academic requirements for entry. The institutions mentioned above are by no means all of those that offer relevant courses.

More details on these and other courses can be obtained by referring to the reference books on courses held by all reference and institution libraries, or to local authority careers officers.

As to the work after training, that is varied and becoming ever more so. Many individuals become self-employed, gaining commissions or undertaking repairs often as much through reputation as through formal advertising. Close contact with relevant bodies is obviously useful – the maker of early instruments will stay in touch with early music groups, university music departments and the like. Piano-tuners will contact schools, private teachers, professional pianists, music shops (retailers often give the first tuning free) and so on.

Some prefer to work with individual companies which range from family firms who have been making one type of instrument for generations to multi-national giants such as Yamaha. Most music reference books carry lists of musical instrument manufacturers – there is also a list in Yellow Pages.

17

Music therapy

There has been a great deal of progress recently in the use of music as a form of therapy for a range of mental and physical disabilities, from autism to deafness, from mental disturbance to physical handicap. There is also a place for music teachers working with children with special needs. The therapy may include both performance and listening, and can involve conventional instruments and compositions, as well as materials designed specifically for such work. The therapy is based on the fact that people who have difficulty in communicating in language, or who experience problems relating to their environment, may be able to express themselves through music. The outcome of this therapy can neither be predicted nor guaranteed, but individual problems have been shown to respond positively to the experience of music.

Music therapists operate with a wide range of clients of all ages and with many differing problems such as emotional disturbance, sensory impairment, language disorder and so on. Therapists are employed in hospitals, special schools, community locations and the like.

It is not possible to enter this field without the proper training, and it is important that you feel sure of your commitment before embarking on such training. Talk to professional people who can help you understand just what the work consists of and what types of jobs are available. There are four one-year full-time training courses in the UK run by the Guildhall School of Music and Drama, the City University, Roehampton Institute of Higher Education and the Nordoff-Robbins Music Therapy Centre in London. Students are normally accepted only if they have had a three-year musical training leading to a degree or diploma from a university or college of music. Further information is available from the above four institutions, as well as from the Association of Professional Music Therapists and the British Society for Music Therapy.

Association of Professional Music Therapists, The Meadow, 68 Pierce Lane, Fulbourn, Cambridge CB1 5DL

British Society for Music Therapy, 69 Avondale Avenue, East Barnet, Herts EN4 8NB

18

Community music

Community music is a very recent approach to music in our society, although in many ways it takes us back to medieval times when the musician was often one of the people, rather than a separate specialist.

Music in the community can take many different forms, and you will find that what counts as community music in one part of the country does not exist elsewhere, or if it does, it may go under a different name, perhaps being part of music education, or part of the work of the social services department, rather than a separate institution. Community music activities can take place in hospitals, old people's homes, youth clubs, community centres, schools and specially built premises.

Generally what links these activities together is an 'everyone can play' approach to music. This can be expressed in two ways. Some community musicians hold the view that being non-elitist means playing the music the people want to hear rather than what you (the 'expert') think they ought to hear. This approach can result in groups of musicians playing songs from 60 years ago to people in an old people's home. Others argue that this is not enough – to be truly non-elitist musical activity should involve all participants equally – no one should be 'on stage'; everyone should share equally in the creation of the musical experience. This can lead community music into a form of music education, with the community musician teaching others to play an instrument, often without reference to written music.

The problem with finding employment in this area of music, either as an administrator or a practitioner, is a lack of funding for such schemes. Some community music is funded by colleges of further and higher education, some by trusts, some by education authorities, but often life is a financial struggle with everyone involved earning far less than they might in other areas of musical work. Certainly it is not normal for anyone to move into community music unless they share a feeling that everyone should have the opportunity to share in music without having undergone a long and rigorous training programme.

Introducing Community Music

As an example of how music in the community can flourish, it is worth looking at an organization known appropriately enough as

Community Music, which described itself as 'London's premier comprehensive music education, training and information resource offering a wide range of services to the community as a whole, in particular to those disadvantaged groups who would not normally get the chance to receive professional musical guidance'.

Community Music runs a workshop training course for the

previously unemployed, an outreach team working in schools, nurseries, centres for people with special needs, drug rehabilitation centres, groups for the elderly, community groups and youth clubs. It also acts as a consultancy service, helping new music projects establish themselves, and passing on information about all areas of musical activity to London's amateur and professional musicians.

About 200 musicians are employed at Community Music, with funding coming from the MSC (now the Training Commission), British Petroleum, Greater London Arts, London Borough Grants Scheme, Calouste Gulbenkian Foundation, Performing Right Society and other sources.

The number of courses and events that Community Music organizes is massive, but I would single out one – Do It Now! – a free music information service which puts tutors and pupils in touch with each other, likewise puts musicians in touch with each other for all types of bands and ensembles, and acts as an information centre for all types of independent music projects, societies, organizations, small record labels and the like. Do It Now! even holds lists of music shops for those who want to buy, rent or have instruments repaired.

By way of contrast you may wish to look at the post-diploma courses for performing musicians at the Guildhall School of Speech and Drama in London, which cover everything from advanced conducting to jazz and rock.

Of course if you are not in London you may well be saying, 'What is the use of all this to me?' There are two answers. Firstly, time and again in this book I have emphasized the fact that to get work in most areas of music you need contacts – you need to be in touch with the music scene in your area. Community projects, such as the one described above, are the perfect way of doing this, if at present you feel left outside the local musical environment. If you have skills to offer, then offer them through a community music centre. If you don't have skills, then you can use such an organization to learn.

But what if there is no community music project in your area? This is where the second alternative comes in. Why not get together with a few friends and start organizing such a project? You may perhaps decide to visit a flourishing community organization to see exactly how such things are arranged. You will need someone who can start the round of asking for money – recruit a financial adminstrator, or become one yourself! You can get in touch with all local groups that are undertaking community work, even if it is not community music work, and gradually expand your level of contacts. You may also feel the need to be trained in this complex and demanding work.

Whichever way you look at it, there is a whole world out there waiting for you. If you are sitting at home waiting for them to come to you, nothing will happen. *Go out and make it happen – now!*

19
On matters of finance

Standard contracts and agreements

Although the inexperienced musician or teacher of music may find him- or herself unsure of how much to charge for a specific job of work, there is a set of contracts which is generally agreed between the major employers and the organizations set up to look after the interests of those working in music. For school and college teachers there should be no problem; the government lays down the salaries to be paid. All state-run institutions are then obliged to stick to them. In effect, most private institutions also accept these rates and pay their staff accordingly.

On this basis, it is possible to work out the going hourly rate for a teacher thus: the average school music teacher works 200 days a year and seven hours a day (including regular commitments to rehearsing the school choir and so on). Assuming that the average yearly salary of an inexperienced music teacher is £8,000, this gives an hourly rate of around £5.71. However, the private teacher is only paid for lessons taught and so should aim to earn around double this rate. A second way to find out the going rate in education is to look at how much adult evening classes pay their lecturers per hour. Also, the Incorporated Society of Musicians has its own standard forms of agreement for private music tuition and can advise its members.

Outside education most negotiations are handled by the Musicians' Union, whose agreements cover such activities as working with the BBC, working for commercial radio and television stations, making records, playing in ballrooms, and so on. However, there may also be occasions when musicians will need to discuss matters with the British Academy of Songwriters, Composers and Authors, the Composers' Guild of Great Britain, Equity, the Association of Professional Recording Studios, or any one of a number of other interested organizations. The general point to remember about conditions of work and payment is that it is all too easy to start by overworking yourself and undercharging for your services. You will then find it very difficult to increase your rates later on. You should always work out what you will actually need to live on, and then pitch your charges accordingly.

GETTING JOBS IN MUSIC

Taxation

In setting oneself up as a freelance, probably the last thing one thinks about is the Inland Revenue. However, rest assured that at some time they, and possibly their colleagues in the Department of Health and Social Security and Customs and Excise, will think about you. Thus it is important from the very start to organize your affairs in such a way that you end up paying as little tax as is legally possible. It is not possible in a book of this nature to discuss tax in great detail, but the following facts may help the newcomer to self-employment to start off in the right direction.

As already suggested, the ideal time to start your self-employment is when either you or your spouse is earning and paying tax in some other occupation. Under these circumstances you can receive a tax allowance for any losses you incur in setting up your own business. Such losses can arise because you have to buy various items of equipment, some of which are allowable for tax purposes, or perhaps you have to spend money promoting yourself by, for example, having publicity photographs taken or advertising in professional journals. In fact, in order to become known you may have to play at concerts, etc., for such low fees that you actually lose money.

Once you have started to work as a freelancer, you will find that you are invariably paying tax in arrears. That is, you pay tax on your earnings for the previous year. Because it always takes a while to sort out one's tax position, it is often the case that one can receive a tax bill some six months after the year in question has ended. Here is how it works in practice. An individual can elect to start his tax year from any date he likes. Let us assume that a musician has a tax year from 6 April to 5 April. On 5 April 1990, he totals up all the money he has earned between 6 April 1989 and 5 April 1990. Next, he writes down all the money he has spent on his business as a musician. This can only include money spent wholly and exclusively on the profession and may include items like printed music, records, petrol, train fares, clarinet reeds, and so on. Most of these items would be immediately allowable against tax, as would such expenses as lighting and heating in a part of the house used exclusively for business (for example, as a practice room or a room for teaching students), clothes such as dress suits or long gowns bought and used exclusively for performance, agents' fees and bank charges on a loan for buying a new instrument. Some items of expenditure would not be allowed, such as a meal bought for an agent or the cost of purchasing a musical instrument which would count as a capital expense which may be allowable against tax at a rate of 25 per cent per year. Over all, the situation would resolve itself like this:

Income	£10,000
Allowable expenses	£6,000
Money spent on capital items 25%	£1,000
Therefore, profit on which tax must be paid	£3,000

The Inland Revenue, if they agree your calculations, will then ask you for the tax due on £3,000, after taking into account your personal allowance.

If you are determined to be self-employed, the best thing to do is keep every receipt for every purchase you make, noting briefly the nature of the expense, file them carefully in date order and, at the end of the tax year, hand your records over to an accountant and ask him to claim the appropriate amount. Then make sure you put aside a sum ready to pay the tax next year.

Further Reading

British Music Education Yearbook, edited by Marianne Barton and Jacqueline Fowler, published by Rhinegold.

Essential reference for anyone thinking of studying music and for those who wish to make a living from teaching. Listings from exam boards to music publishers, independent schools offering music scholarships to colleges of music. Four hundred pages of accurate information.

British Music Yearbook, edited by Marianne Barton, published by Rhinegold.

Definitive book of addresses and information for all musicians except perhaps the out and out rockers. Associations, societies, studios, folk agencies, jazz festivals and much much more. Should be on every professional's shelf.

Kemps International Music and Recording Industry Yearbook, published by Kemps.

Detailed listings of all aspects of music. The concert section, for example, contains listings of concert and tour co-ordinators, managers and promoters, all manner of equipment, transport companies, and a very large list of venues. Should be in most reference libraries.

Music Week Directory, edited by David Dalton, published by
Spotlight Publications.

Well-established directory from the leading trade magazine, with
listings from booking agents to computer services, mobile studios to
music publishers. Like *Kemps* should be in all reference libraries.
Complain if it isn't.

The Musician's Handbook, edited by Trevor Ford, published by
Rhinegold.

Interesting series of articles on earning a living and building a career
in music. A marked emphasis on classical work, but the financial
section will be of use to all musicians.

Acknowledgements

The author and publishers thank the following for permission to reproduce
illustrations:
pp. 12, 42 The Purcell School (photographs by Jennifer Ransom Carter);
p. 15 Lawrence Perkins;
p. 20 D.K. Wilson, Head of Performing Arts and Media Studies, Salford College
of Technology;
pp. 23, 36 Graham Wade, City of Leeds College of Music;
p. 36 Colin R. Buck, Studio 81, Darlington;
p. 75 Norman Divall, Capital Radio;
pp. 77, 81 CBS Records;
p. 91 W.H. Smith Group, Public Relations Department;
p. 94 Quadrivium (photographed by Fritz Curzon);
p. 102 West Dean College (photographs by Paul Biddle);
p. 107 Kilby, Hastings.